SWEDISH SWEATERS

NEW DESIGNS FROM HISTORICAL EXAMPLES

BRITT-MARIE CHRISTOFFERSSON

SWEDISH SWEATERS

NEW DESIGNS FROM HISTORICAL EXAMPLES

TRANSLATED BY GUNNEL MELCHERS

The Taunton Press

The front-cover illustration shows a
sweater called *Jolly* (see p. 79).

Photos by Anders Rising, except at follows:
p. 31, left: R. Hejdström
p. 29, p. 47: The Nordic Museum, Stockholm
Publication designer: Johan Ogden
Layout and mounting of original text: Reklam-Montage AB, Eskilstuna

© 1990 by The Taunton Press, Inc.
All rights reserved

First printing: October 1990

First published in Sweden by
ICA bökforlag
Stora gatan 41
721 85 Västerås
SWEDEN

Printed in West Germany

The Taunton Press
63 South Main Street
Box 5506
Newtown, CT 06470-5506

Library of Congress Cataloging-in-Publication Data

Christoffersson, Britt-Marie.
   [Svenska tröjor. English]
   Swedish Sweaters : New designs from historical examples / Britt-Marie
Christoffersson. : translated by Gunnel Melchers.
   p. cm. — (International craft classic)
   Translation of: Svenska tröjor.
   ISBN 0-942391-80-2 : $15.95
   1. Sweaters. 2. Knitting — Patterns. I. Title. II. Series.
TT825.C42313   1990   90-11129
746.9'2 — dc20   CIP

Table of Contents

Introduction

Professionally speaking, the 1980s turned out — somewhat unexpectedly — to be an exciting decade for me. I was trained as a designer in the mid-1960s, when our chief concern was keeping track of the never-ending flood of new products and creating some kind of meaning and content in our work. The product became more important than the designer, and rather than the choice of a number of variations on the same theme in fashion, the prospective customer was to have access to a virtually unlimited selection of patterns and designs: from plain colors, delicate prints and checked and striped patterns to the unexpected and fantastic.

The trend shift around 1980 brought a shift of values in the professional designers' world, as expressed by a design critic: "Function changed into imagination, demand into desire." As I see it, however, all four concepts should be kept alive at the same time, and although a great deal of the new fashion appealed to me, something seemed to be lacking.

Simultaneously, another trend stole up on me: the knitting boom in the 1980s. Knitting had always been a hobby of mine, but then I took up a serious study of it and was truly fascinated. I knitted samples by following descriptions of various techniques found in Swedish and foreign literature. It was not long before I had several hundred samples, and I had the happy feeling of having increased my knowledge at the same rate. In fact, I felt that I had acquired expert knowledge in the same way as I had with other textile techniques during my training at the Borås Textile Institute and the College for Design and Craft in Stockholm. Not surprisingly, then, I began to wonder why I had never been given this knowledgeable approach to knitting during my training as a textile designer. Why was knowledge of the history and techniques of knitting not seen as useful as those of weaving and embroidery? Is the general idea that there is no knowledge to be acquired beyond the ability to cast on stitches and to knit or purl them? During the 1980s it was stated often enough that knitting should be part and parcel of designer training, and I certainly subscribe to that view. It would benefit the training of designers as well as the development and quality of the knitting craft itself.

As I sat surrounded by all my swatches, I realized what a good thing it was to have knitted them. In realizing that, I envisioned a more specific use for the swatches: I would put together study material on knitting. The technical details were illustrated by means of the swatches; the next step was a demonstration of traditional Swedish knitting. A grant from the Artists' Council gave me the chance to travel around the country visiting museums and copying old knitting patterns. These were then knitted up into samples for the purpose of imparting knowledge of the imagination and skill that characterized knitters in the old days.

These swatches and samples, showing technical possibilities and traditional patterns, became a traveling exhibition called "Old Patterns, New Sweaters, Worldwide Knitting Techniques," which has been shown in museums and craft shops since the autumn of 1985. In connection with the exhibition I have given courses, using the material for study purposes.

A recurring question during these courses has been what made me so interested in knitting. I think the main reason is my fascination for patterns. What arouses my interest in particular is the actual craftsmanship, the folk art, the anonymous, nondesigned objects. Increasingly, I have begun to feel more at home in a museum filled with objects manufactured out of need, yet beautifully decorated, than in metropolitan showrooms.

Craftwork and craftsmanship are of great importance, more than ever in this time of quickly developing high technology. Were it not for the practicing craftspeople who keep working against all odds, this kind of activity might well be in danger of extinction. Taxes and duties of various kinds have made craftwork products into luxury articles, and the craftsman has to struggle for professional survival. Yet I do sense that there is a great interest in craftwork and that it is an important hobby for many people. The fact that knitting does not have a very high standing compared with other crafts is partly explained by our general insistence on finishing a knitted garment in great hurry, which is somewhat unfortunate. The interest is focused on the finished sweater, not on the process itself and the experience and knowledge that it may impart. I cannot emphasize enough what a stimulating, important and worthwhile craft knitting can be.

At this point I would like to relate what I learned from listening to Gunnar Arnborg, a teacher at a Swedish folk high school, who recently — in a radio program — gave an account of a visit to a certain Alfred Andersson of Källeryd in the province of Västergötland. Accompanied by a group of students, Arnborg paid a visit to this man for the purpose of getting familiar with and documenting the craftwork that used to be carried out at the local farms. This documentation resulted in a publication called *Hemmagjort (Homemade)*. While visiting Alfred Andersson, the group was shown, among other things, a fine adjustable dressing mirror. Arnborg then discussed the complicated nature of Andersson's work with his students: "He made the mirror in the most complicated manner conceivable, making turned pieces to hold it. Not only were the pieces turned, but they were turned in spirals, which was much more difficult than turning straight pieces. In addition, the mirror featured cut-out garlands, embossed drawers and other elaborate details." The visitors asked Andersson why he made things so difficult for himself — after all, he could have made a mirror in a much simpler way. Arnborg related: "The answer was obvious. Being a true craftsman he knew that the more difficult he made it for himself, the more use he made of his skill and the more he developed his craftsmanship. If he had chosen the other direction and made it easier and easier for himself, it would have had a shrinking effect on him as a man." Arnborg adds: "This seems to me to bear on our most important cultural issue. If we lead our lives in such a way that we make less and less use of our potentials, we shrink. If, on the other hand, we make demands, impart hopes and enthusiasm and want a bit more, we are on the right track."

Such is the way I wish craftwork, including knitting, was viewed today. In the push-button society that is not just facing us but in which, to some extent, we already live, craftwork may become an area where human curiosity and creativity are satisfied. In everyday life and work, automation will ensure that only a few people — those who develop and program the computers — will satisfy their need for creativity. It could be, in fact, that crafts for hobby activities and small-scale production will become a compelling necessity for human survival in a high-technology society.

This book is based on my study material as described above; however, it has not been possible to include all the material within the framework of a normal-sized book. In *Swedish Sweaters,* then, I decided to display a number of historical garments and nearly as many contemporary ones to illustrate how my work has been inspired by the old traditions and techniques.

The 27 historical garments presented in this book were all knitted during the latter half of the 19th century, with one or two exceptions. They are characterized by having been knitted from thin, tightly spun yarn. Today these garments make a somewhat stiff impression. The fact that they lack the elasticity so characteristic of knitting has to do with the woven textures that served as models; the elastic potential of knitwear had not yet been discovered. However, using the old patterns for a so-called quick-and-easy sweater knitted from thick yarn with thick needles does no

justice to the model. In fact, it might well make the patterns disproportionate and ugly.

It has not been my intention to give guidance for direct copying of the historical garments. That tradition is kept up by people living in the areas where the garments originate. Rather, the sweaters in the first part of the book should be seen as sources of inspiration for present-day design. What the left-hand pages show are the most important elements of the patterns; they do not provide charts and diagrams for the knitting of a complete garment.

The second part of the book shows how the historical sweaters have inspired me in designing new models. Sometimes the step from the historical to the contemporary is so short that it needs no explanation. Sometimes, however, it is so large and so many links in the chain of association are missing that the historical garment hardly seems to relate to the new design at all — yet it always does. The sweaters often exemplify what fascinated me most of all when working with patterns: the utmost simplicity as well as the combination of many patterns.

My work is no attempt to meddle with the making of traditional garments. I do not intend to create a Delsbo or Järvsö sweater for the 1990s, but rather sweaters for everyday use, where tradition is only part of the garment's character.

Since it is not my wish to make the sweaters appear stiff and awkward or to deform or misrepresent the historical patterns, I have tried to strike a happy medium in using knitting needles in sizes 2mm, 2½mm, 3mm,

3½mm and 4mm (equal to U.S. sizes 0, 1-2, 2-3, 4 and 5-6; U.K. sizes 14, 12-13, 11, 9-10 and 8). This type of garment is based on a plain yarn; it is the pattern and not the appearance of the yarn that is the important thing. The stitches should be subordinate to the pattern, which demands quite tight knitting. I often like to use weaving yarn, especially when I ply several colors together to form a multicolored strand. This plied yarn may call for an explanation, since it is often perceived as prickly. To me the color is all important when I design a garment, and I have not succeeded in finding (in Sweden) a soft, neutral commercial 2-ply or 3-ply yarn in a wide color range. If I am to make a multicolored sweater, I have difficulty in subordinating myself even to a superior quality of yarn if it does not offer a wide selection of colors. If I mix yarn from various spinning mills, the plied yarn provides me with a gigantic range of colors. With respect to its prickliness, it is somewhat comforting that a garment knitted in plied yarn becomes softer after washing. You may also find that you enjoy working these patterns with Shetland yarn (see the listing of suppliers on p. 141).

Strangely enough, considering that the purpose of the book has been to show the historical patterns as a source of inspiration, I have had no use for my original swatches that document the old techniques.

I cherish the hope that more and more people will be able to design their knitted garments themselves. It is so rewarding not to be inhibited by a fixed pattern but rather to acquire knowledge and to use one's potential creativity to enjoy the process of knitting as much as the finished garment. To all of you interested in knitting: take a course, do your own thinking, help each other, keep trying new things, knit swatches, undo your knitting and start again! Make it just as difficult for yourself as you want it to be. It can be quite a challenge.

If the contemporary sweaters, like the historical, can function as a source of inspiration for those of you who make your own designs, I have been successful in yet another aim in writing this book.

Swedish Sweaters has been created from the point of view of a designer, not an ethnologist or a purely practical person. It does not contain a word about the knowledge of materials or instructions for design, finishing and care; nor does it contain a history of knitting. I preferred to fill the pages with historical and contemporary sweaters.

Now that *Swedish Sweaters* is available in the bookshops, the knitting boom of the 1980s is past history. As I see it, it is all the better that the book is published at such a time. A craft that is taken seriously can never be out of fashion, and during my involvement with the traveling exhibition I realized that there are many people with a firmly rooted interest in craftwork and knitting who remain untouched by the ups and downs of fashion.

1

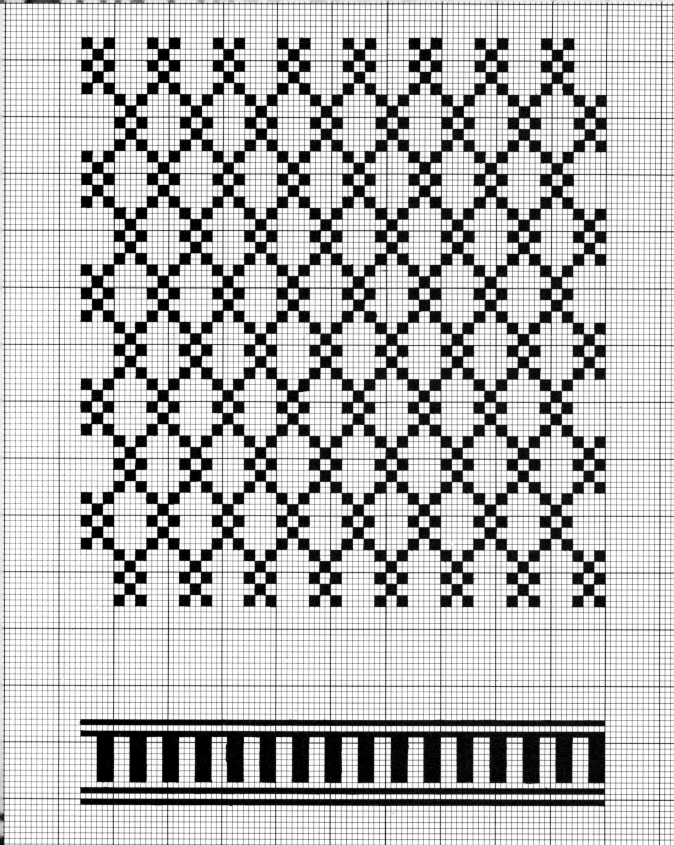

Woman's Sweater from Skåne

A textured sweater know as *spedetröja*, where purl stitches form a relief pattern against the plain background. The sweater is decorated with multicolored ribbons around the wrists.

Gauge: 39-42 stitches to 10cm/4 in.

□ = knit stitch
■ = purl stitch

The Ystad Greyfriar Monastery (Gråbrödraklostret)

Woman's Sweater from the Oxie District, Skåne

A *spedetröja* in textured knitting, decorated with green fabric.

Gauge: 41 stitches to 10cm/4 in.

□ = knit stitch
■ = purl stitch

The Malmö Museum

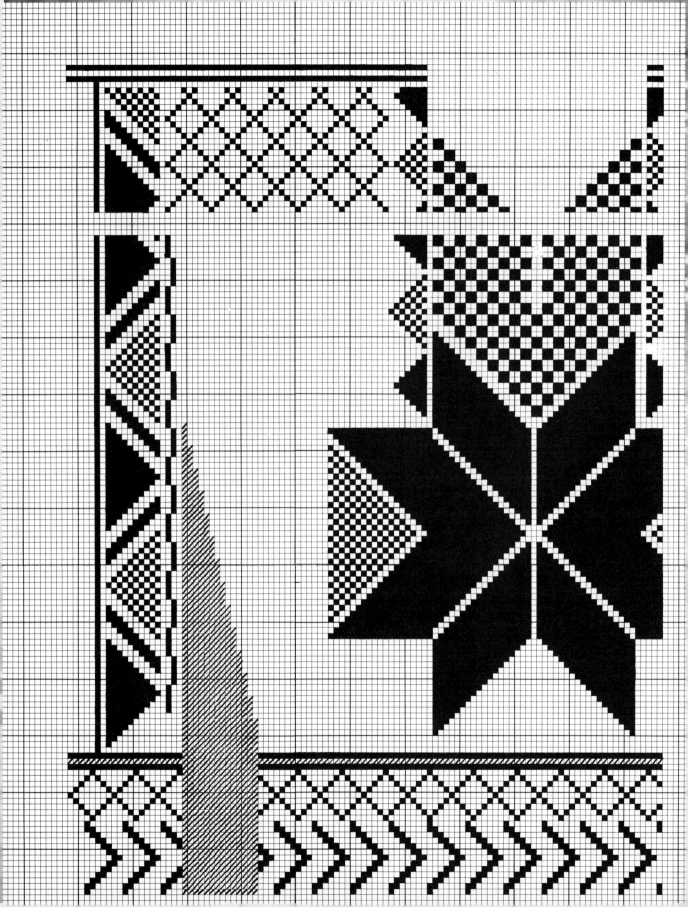

Woman's Sweater from the Luggude District, Skåne

A *spedetröja* in textured knitting, decorated with green silk and chain-stitch embroidery around the neck and woven ribbons around the wrists. Note the beautifully worked increases in the bodice.

Gauge: 42 stitches to 10cm/4 in.

☐ = knit stitch
■ = purl stitch
/ = no stitch, shows increase in width

The Helsingborg Museum

Woman's Sweater from Tönnersjö Parish, Halland

A sweater in textured knitting. Purl stitches form a pattern against the plain (knit) background. This is probably the oldest garment shown in this book. It is made of cotton yarn and has been knitted in the round. Where a corresponding garment manufactured by sewing would have a side seam, this sweater has a simple pattern marking: a textured square knitted over 2 stitches and 2 rounds alternating with 2 plain rounds. It also features sleeve gussets.

Gauge: 53 stitches to 10cm/4 in.

□ = knit stitch
■ = purl stitch

Inset in the lower right-hand corner: chart for the lower end (the welt) of the sleeve.

The Halmstad Museum

19

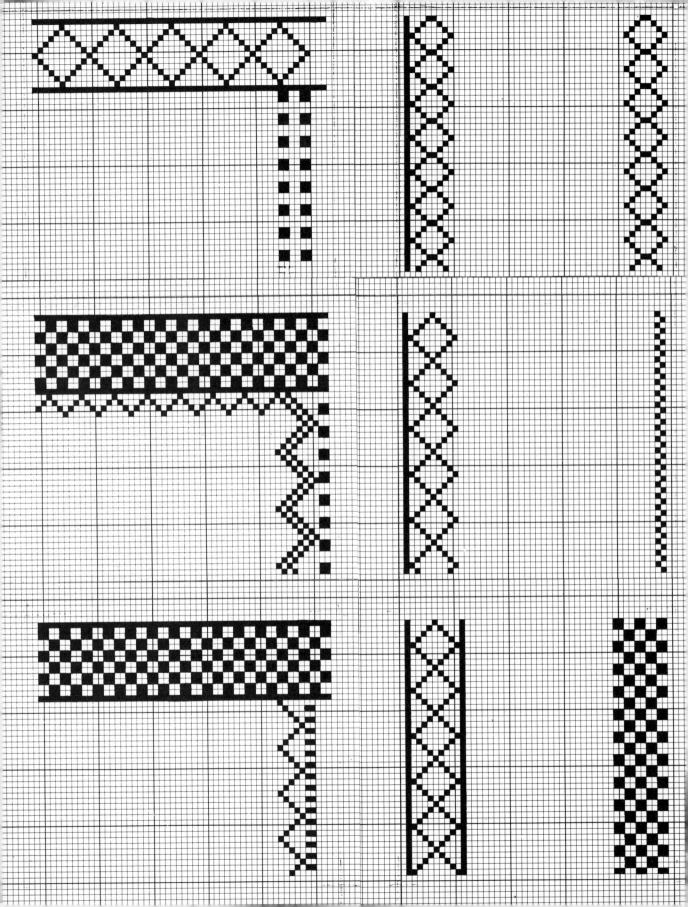

Woman's Sweater from Halland

A sweater knitted in stockinette stitch, except for the textured patterns in purl stitches indicated by the photograph and the diagrams at the top of the facing page. The other diagrams show the patterns of two similar garments.

Gauge: 36 stitches to 10cm/4 in.

□ = knit stitch
■ = purl stitch

The Halmstad Museum

Man's Sweater from Halland

The sweater is knitted in two-color stockinette stitch in what is known as the Bjärbo pattern. Note the reversed triangles of the "side seam," which divide the front and back at the armhole.

Gauge: 32 stitches to 10cm/4 in.

□ = green
■ = red

The welt is knitted in garter stitch; a row of squares in the diagram corresponds to two knitted rows. The first six rows are knitted in green.

The Varberg Museum

Man's Sweater from the Village of Sjö, Halland

Stockinette stitch in two colors. The cast-on technique that gives the red edge is known as "twisted cast-on," where two strands of different colors are used for casting on. In this case, loops of the red strand have been picked up from the left thumb. The striped rib is made up of knit stitches alternating with purl.

Inset in the lower left-hand corner on the facing page: pattern for the sleeve.

Gauge: 31 stitches to 10cm/4 in. for the rib
33 stitches to 10cm/4 in. for the stockinette stitch

□ = red
■ = black

The Halmstad Museum

Man's Sweater from Hishult, Halland

Stockinette stitch in two colors. The rib is made up of 2 black knit stitches alternating with 2 red purl stitches. The "seams," which are knitted over 5 stitches in this sweater, are of practical use in circular knitting; it is possible to avoid the dislocation of patterns that tends to occur when a new round is begun. If, as in this case, increases are made for the width of the sleeve, they are placed between the "seam" and the other stitches.

Inset in the lower left-hand corner on the facing page: pattern for the sleeve.

Gauge: 33 stitches to 10cm/4 in.

□ = red
■ = black
/ = no stitch, shows increase in sleeve width

The Varberg Museum

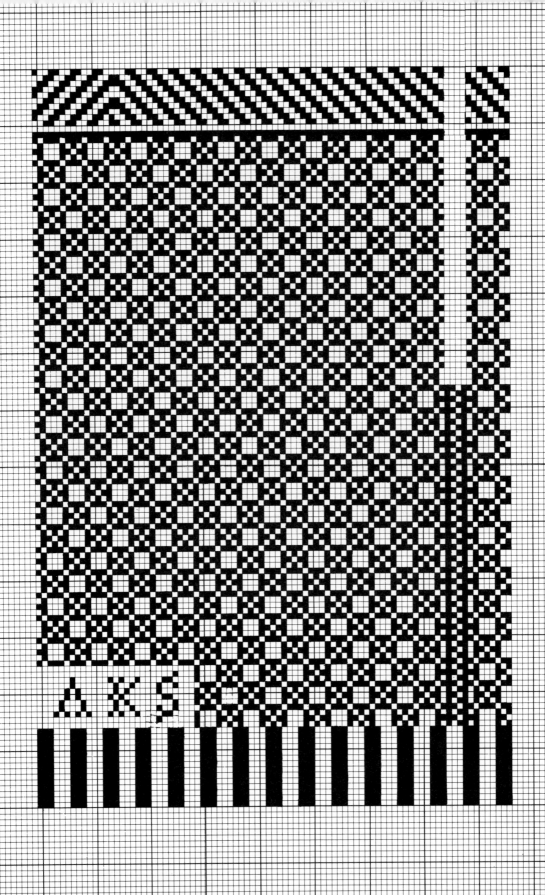

Man's Sweater from Sotenäs, Bohuslän

Stockinette stitch in two colors. The rib is made up of 3 red knit stitches alternating with 3 blue purl stitches. The sweater is knitted from top to bottom. In casting off, blue and red strands have been used alternately.

Gauge: 42 stitches to 10cm/4 in.

□ = red
■ = blue

The Nordic Museum, Stockholm

Pattern for the Patchwork Leg of the Stocking

Using black yarn, cast on 2 stitches.
Row 1: Purl 2.
Row 2: Increase to 3 stitches and knit these.
Row 3: Purl 3.
Row 4: Increase, knit 4.
Row 5: Purl 4.
Row 6: Increase, knit 5.
Row 7: Purl 5.
Row 8: Increase, knit 6.
Row 9: Purl 6.
Row 10: Increase, knit 7.
Row 11: Purl 7.
Row 12: Increase, knit 8.
Row 13: Purl 8.

This completes the first half of the top square. Leave it on the left needle. Do not cut the yarn off. Cast on 2 stitches, knit these and repeat rows 1-13. Continue in this way until there are 8 half-squares on the left needle. Knit an additional row on the last square. Do not cut the yarn off.

An alternate method is to cast on the number of stitches needed for the size of the garment; for the stocking this would amount to 8 stitches, for 8 squares make 64 stitches. The stitches are then included in the knitting, using short rows, according to the increase rate described above.

Using a third needle and red yarn, pick up 8 stitches along the left side of the last square.

Row 1: Purl 8 (the new red stitches).
Row 2: Knit 7, knit together the last stitch with the nearest black stitch from the square to the left, knitting into the backs of the stitches.
Row 3: Slip 1, purl 7.
Row 4: Knit 7, knit 2 together as in Row 2. Continue until there are no more stitches in the black half square. Then pick up 8 red stitches along the side of that square and continue knitting as before. While knitting, distribute the stitches over an appropriate number of needles for knitting in the round.

The stitches of the 8th red square are knitted together with the square farthest to the right, i.e., the knitting is to be circular. Knit an additional row on the last square. Do not cut the yarn off.

Using black yarn, pick up 8 stitches at the place where the yarn had been left hanging and continue knitting. The "rounds of squares" are knitted clockwise and counterclockwise alternately. Sometimes the squares are knitted together from the back, i.e., 2 purl stitches together without deviation from the normal procedure. Sometimes the new stitches are picked up with the back of the knitting facing the knitter. Then put the needle in from the front side, pulling the yarn from the back through.

Except for the half squares, the stocking consists of 11 rounds of 8-stitch squares. Then follow 8 rounds of 7-stitch squares, and at the bottom, 4 rounds of 6-stitch squares. The decreases are made by picking up one stitch less. In the process of knitting stitches together, 1 stitch may be knitted together with 2 from the preceding square.

Half squares before proceeding to the knitting of the foot: Pick up stitches for a new square as before. At the side of the square where the knitting together is not done, decrease 1 stitch at the beginning of the row. An alternative method is to leave some stitches unknitted on the needle as you go along.

Woman's Sweater and Stocking from Gotland

This type of sweater or cardigan, known as *källingtröja,* is knitted in fisherman's rib. Both the front pieces have a border (button band) knitted in garter stitch and with a zigzag eyelet pattern.

Gotlands Fornsal, Visby

The knitting technique used in the stocking is called diagonal patchwork knitting (entrelac or interlaced) or "birch-bark knapsack knitting." It has been used for stockings and mittens in various parts of Sweden.

Gotlands Fornsal, Visby

Woman's Sweater from Gagnef and Knitted Sleeve from Enviken, Dalarna

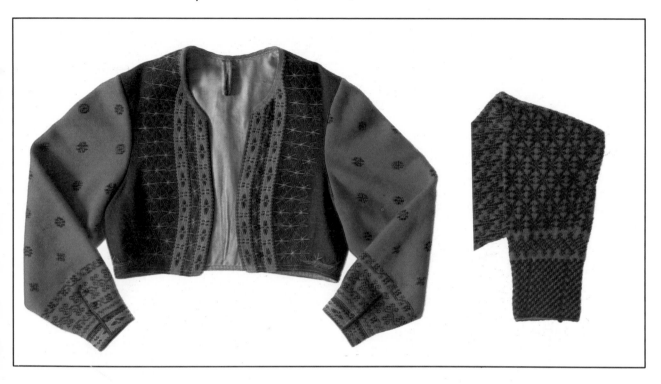

The front and back pieces of the bodice are made of thick, homespun cloth *(vadmal)*. The sleeves are done in two-strand (twined) knitting. They were knitted in natural white and black and later dyed red. The number of pattern types around the sleeve is constant. Increases in the width of the sleeve are distributed over the rows, so that the distance between the patterns grows as the sleeve gets wider.

Gauge: 53 stitches to 10cm/4 in.

□ = red
■ = black

See the diagram on the left side of the facing page.

The Museum of Dalarna, Falun

Gauge: About 40 stitches to 10cm/4 in.

□ = red
■ = black

See the diagram on the right side of the facing page.

The Museum of Dalarna, Falun

Sweater from Dala-Floda, Dalarna

The front and back pieces are made of *vadmal* cloth. The sleeves are done in two-strand (twined) black-and-white knitting and were later dyed red.

□ = red
■ = black
/ = no stitch, shows increase in sleeve width

The Museum of Dalarna, Falun

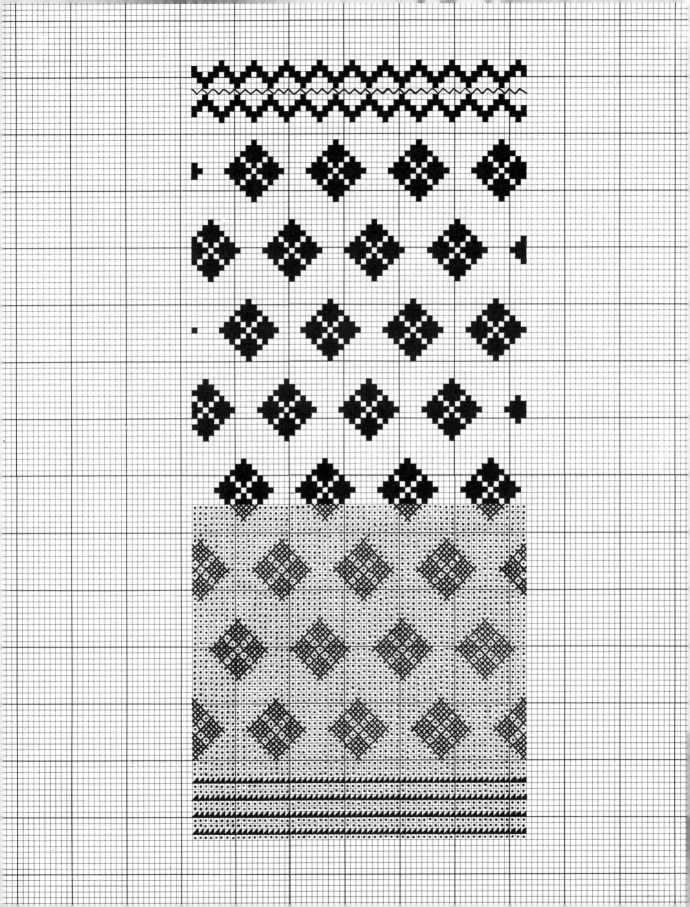

Woman's Sweater from Forsa, Hälsingland

The bottom, lighter part of the sweater is done in two-strand (twined) knitting, while the top part is done in ordinary two-color knitting.

Gauge: 38 stitches to 10cm/4 in.

● = light red
× = light green
□ = red
■ = green
▲ = two-stranded purl stitches, floating on the front side
V = simultaneous knitting together and casting off of back and front shoulder stitches

The Museum of Hälsingland, Hudiksvall

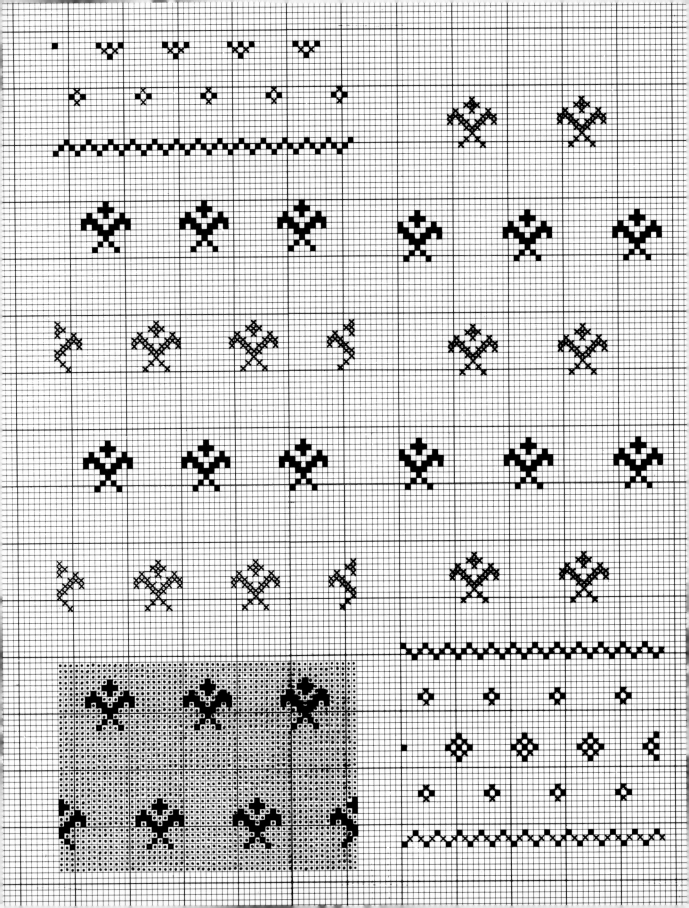

Woman's Sweater from Järvsö, Hälsingland

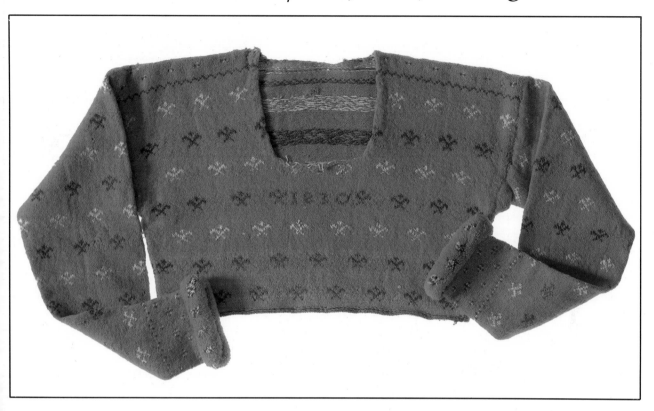

This stockinette-stitch sweater was knitted in 1830.

Gauge: 40 stitches to 10cm/4 in.

● = light red
□ = red
■ = green
× = pale yellow

The diagram on the facing page shows the pattern of the front and back pieces (left) and the pattern of the sleeve (lower right).

The Museum of Hälsingland, Hudiksvall

Woman's Sweater from Järvsö, Hälsingland

This stockinette-stitch sweater was knitted in 1838.

Gauge: 40 stitches to 10cm/4 in.

× = reddish pink
□ = red
■ = black
● = green

The diagram on the facing page shows the patterns of the front and back pieces (left) and those of the sleeve (right). The pattern of the sleeve gusset is shown in the top right-hand corner. The gusset is knitted as a triangular-shaped insert of the sleeve for the purpose of increased comfort. One side of the triangle is sewn on to the front piece, the other to the back piece.

Private property.

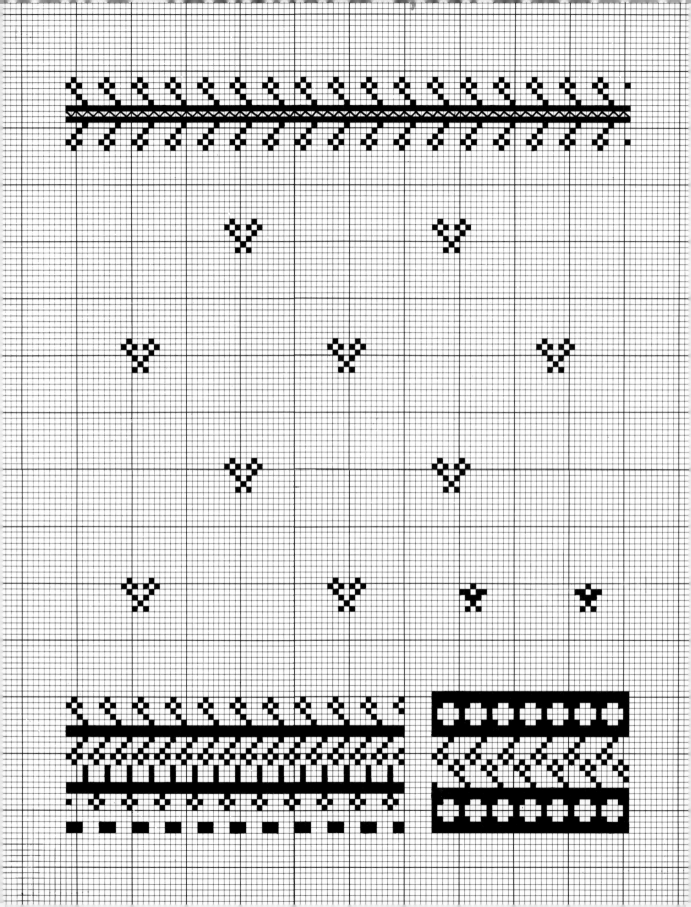

Woman's Sweater from Ljusdal, Hälsingland

This sweater is done in two-strand (twined) knitting. Note the particularly beautiful finishing at the shoulder.

Gauge: 50 stitches to 10cm/4 in.

□ = red
■ = green
∨ = simultaneous knitting together and casting off of the front and back shoulder stitches

Inset in the lower right-hand side of the facing page: the border and first pattern type used for the sleeve.

The Museum of Hälsingland, Hudiksvall

Man's Sweater from Ljusdal, Hälsingland

□ = red
■ = green
\ = two-strand purl stitches, red
  and green
V = simultaneous knitting
  together and casting off of
  the front and back shoulder
  stitches

The Museum of Hälsingland,
Hudiksvall

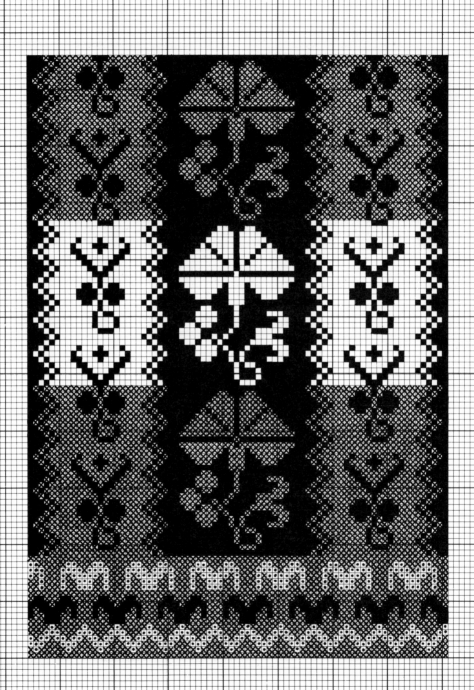

Woman's Sweater from Alfta, Hälsingland

This sweater has knitted sleeves and shoulder pieces; the rest is made of black woolen cloth. The white parts are knitted in cotton yarn.

Gauge: 38 stitches to 10cm/4 in.

× = red
■ = green
● = black
□ = white

The Nordic Museum, Stockholm

Man's Sweater from Ovanåker, Hälsingland

This sweater is knitted in two-color stockinette stitch. Usually, sweaters from Alfta and Ovanåker have only knitted sleeves and shoulder pieces, while the rest of the garment is made of cloth (see the sweater from Alfta on p. 47).

Gauge: 37 stitches to 10cm/4 in.

□ = green
■ = black
/ = two-strand purl stitches, floating on the front side

The Museum of Hälsingland, Hudiksvall

Man's Sweater from Bjuråker, Hälsingland

This stockinette-stitch sweater is knitted in several colors, but never more than two at a time. The white parts are knitted in cotton yarn. The sweater was knitted in 1870.

Gauge: 39 stitches to 10cm/4 in.

□ = white
● = green
✕ = red
■ = black

The Museum of Hälsingland, Hudiksvall

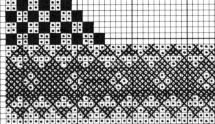

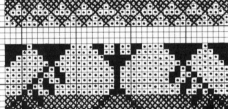

Man's Sweater from Delsbo, Hälsingland

Gauge: 42 stitches to 10cm/4 in.

The Museum of Hälsingland, Hudiksvall

× = red
● = green
■ = black

Man's Sweater from Bjuråker, Hälsingland

This stockinette-stitch sweater is knitted in two colors. It differs from other Bjuråker sweaters, which tend to include more varied patterns and more colors, such as red and white in addition to black and green.

□ = green
■ = black
/ = no stitch, shows increase in width

The diagram on the facing page shows the patterns of the front and back pieces (left) and those of the sleeve (right).

The Bjuråker Folklore Society

Man's Sweater from Älvros, Härjedalen

This sweater was knitted in 1858 by Brita Persson of the Älvros church village. The technique is two-color stockinette stitch. The beautiful pattern of the lower edge is the chain effect resulting from two-strand (twined) knitting.

Gauge: 35-40 stitches to 10cm/4 in.

☐ = red

■ = black

● = black knit (stockinette) stitch. The black yarn is left on the reverse side of the knitting.

– = red purl stitch. The red yarn is left on the front side of the knitting.

The Jämtland Provincial Museum, Östersund

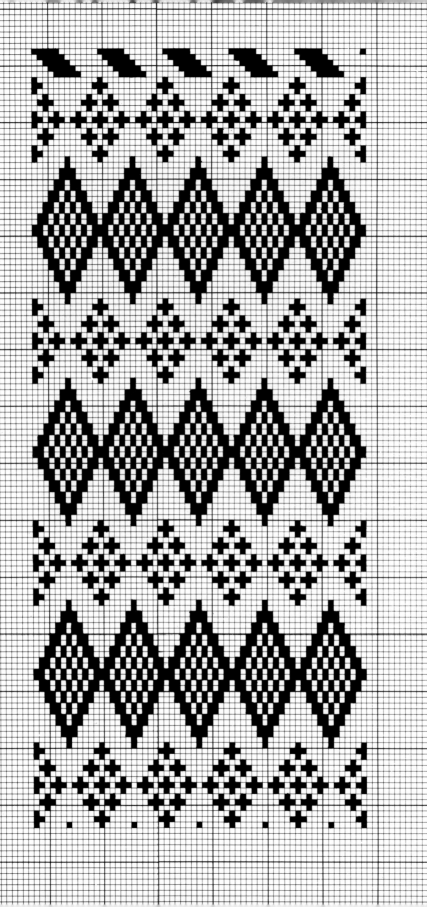

Jacket and Coverlet by Märta Stina Abrahamsdotter

This jacket is knitted in two-color stockinette stitch. It is probably not based on a set model or graphic chart. The various patterns differ in the number of stitches for each repeat, which might lead to certain "clashes" sideways. Märta Stina solved that problem by knitting a few stitches together and making the corresponding increases wherever necessary. As always in her knitting, no strands are visible across the back of the work; they have been knitted in.

The charts refer to the patterns for the sleeves (p. 58), the lower part of the jacket (p. 60) and the upper part of the jacket (p. 61).

Gauge: 35 stitches to 10cm/4 in.

□ = black
■ = red

The Härnösand Provincial Museum

Märta Stina Abrahamsdotter

Märta Stina Abrahamsdotter (1825-1903) lived in the little village of Kubbe, in the Anundsjö parish in the province of Ångermanland. She never married, and on her father's death she became a pauper.

As a young girl she began to knit caps, mittens and sweaters for local people, which provided her with a small income. She always knitted richly patterned garments, which were very impressive with their many colors, high quality and fine technique. The patterns were often inspired by fabrics woven in the rosepath technique, but she also used strict floral designs.

During the last few decades of her life Märta Stina also knitted coverlets, using fairly thick yarn. Like her sweaters, the coverlets are characterized by magnificent patterns. Large heart-shaped designs forming continuous patterns with ingenious mirror effects are filled with squares and diagonals reflected in various directions.

When knitting with two colors, Märta Stina always knitted in the wool not in use at the back of the work by twisting it around the wool in use on every stitch. In order to avoid tangling the yarns she was using, she took the yarn alternately from above and below when changing colors.

It is known that Märta Stina was regarded as slightly crazy. The very fact that she was a dedicated and ingenious knitter may have been one of the reasons why she was considered to be "different."

In 1910, seven years after the death of Märta Stina, her coverlets were displayed at the craft exhibition at Sollefteå, attracting due attention.

Only one of the sweaters Märta Stina knitted appears to have been preserved. As many as 12 coverlets are extant, most of which are kept at the Härnösand Provincial Museum. Two coverlets are to be found at the Nordic Museum in Stockholm, three in the Sollefteå Handicraft Archives, and one has remained on the farm where Märta Stina once lived.

It is worth pointing out the stranded-color knitting was quite unusual in the traditional Ångermanland knitting. Yet Märta Stina knitted these splendid things, and one cannot help being filled with astonishment and admiration.

Coverlet

The coverlet is knitted in two-color plain stockinette stitch. The work has been done in five sections, that is, two side borders and three parts that have been knitted in the round and then cut open; these three pieces make up the middle section. The size of the coverlet is roughly 110cm/43½ in. by 150cm/59 in.

Gauge: 26 stitches to 10cm/4 in.

Horizontal pattern

1: □ = brownish red   ■ = green
2: □ = brownish red   × = purple
3: □ = brownish red   ■ = green
4: □ = brownish red   × = purple
5: □ = brownish red   ■ = green
6: □ = brownish red   × = purple

For charts, see pp. 64-66.

The Härnösand Provincial Museum

2

Dad's Thick Sweater and Mum's Fine One

Dad's Thick Sweater is meant to be a man-sized women's sweater. The idea is that it should look as if it were borrowed from Dad, yet the sleeve length should fit the person who wears the sweater.

The sweater is knitted sideways, from one seam to the other. All borders are knitted on the garment afterwards; these are knitted in stockinette stitch and are all double, i.e., they have been folded. The pattern around the neck is an adaptation of the Scanian textured sweater from Luggude (see p. 17).

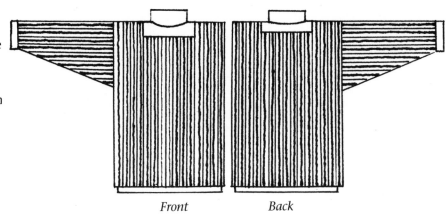

Front   *Back*

Mum's Fine One is knitted in a finer yarn. The pattern is an adaptation from a detail in a Scanian "bridegroom stocking." (The stocking, which is kept at the Ystad Greyfriar Monastery, is not shown in this book.) A characteristic rib is used for this sweater, consisting of 1 knit stitch and 3 stitches knitted in a moss-stitch pattern.

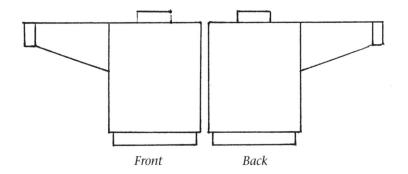

Front   *Back*

Dad's Thick Sweater

MEASUREMENTS (CHEST SIZE)

Small: 112cm/44 in.
(Medium: 126cm/49½ in.)
Large: 138cm/54½ in.

YARN

Sport-weight yarn
11 (12) 13 100g hanks or balls
[36 oz. (40 oz.) 43 oz.]

NEEDLES

1 pair in size 3½mm (U.S. 4, U.K. 9-10), 1 circular needle in size 3 ½mm (U.S. 4, U.K. 9-10) and 1 set of four or five double-pointed needles in size 3½mm (U.S. 4, U.K. 9-10)

GAUGE

24 stitches to 10cm/4 in. It is recommended to knit a gauge sample; should your gauge differ from the one indicated, change to smaller or larger needles.

FRONT

The sweater is knitted sideways, from one seam to the other. Pattern repeat:
Row 1: Knit.
Row 2: Purl.
Row 3: Knit.
Row 4: Knit.
Row 5: Purl.
Row 6: Knit.

Cast on 152 (166) 180 sts. Knit 11½ (14½) 17½ pattern repeats.
   Cast off 24 sts on one side.
   Knit 25½ pattern repeats.
   Cast on 24 sts on the same side as the casting off was done.
   Knit 11½ (14½) 17½ pattern repeats. Cast off.

BACK

Cast on 152 (166) 180 sts. Knit 11½ (14½) 17½ pattern repeats.
   Cast off 18 sts on one side.
   Knit 25½ pattern repeats.
   Cast on 18 sts on the same side as the casting off was done.
   Knit 11½ (14½) 17½ pattern repeats. Cast off.

SLEEVES

Cast on 86 (92) 98 sts. Knit 1 row, then purl 1 row (this is to be the right side of the work), then knit 1 row. Start knitting the pattern as above; however, to create the shape of the sleeve, incorporate the stitches gradually using short rows: knit 2 rows over 6 stitches, then 2 rows over 9 sts, 2 rows over 12 sts, 2 rows over 15 sts, etc., until all stitches have been incorporated.

   Knit 28½ (30½) 32½ pattern repeats. Then decrease the number of working stitches by 3 every other row in order to make the sleeve wide at one end and narrow at the other.

Knit 3 rows in stockinette stitch (with purl stitches on the right side of the work), using all the stitches. Cast off.

FINISHING

Pick up about 32 (37) 42 sts along the shoulders. Knit 3 rows in stockinette stitch, with the purl stitches on the right (front) side.

   Knit the shoulder stitches from the back and front pieces together, casting off at the same time (see p. 115).

   Pick up about 100 (106) 112 sts along the upper end of the sleeve. Knit 3 rows in stockinette stitch, with the purl stitches on the right (front) side. This border will function as the seam allowance when the sleeve is sewn onto the front and back pieces. It is needed on account of the difference in stretching between the two pieces.

NECKBAND

Pick up 65 sts along the front neck. Knit the pattern (see the facing page) and shape the neck, casting off according to the chart. Put the remaining sts on a safety pin or piece of yarn.

   Pick up the same number of stitches and knit the back according to the chart.

   Knit the remaining stitches together, casting off at the same time.

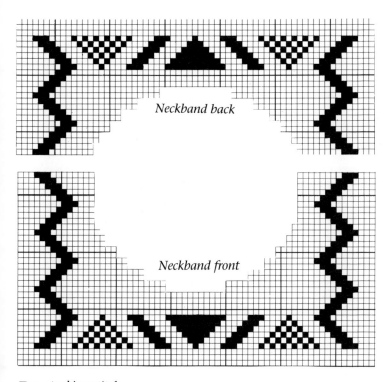

Neckband back

Neckband front

☐ = stocking stitch

■ = purl stitch

TURTLENECK

Pick up about 94 stitches with the double-pointed needles. Knitting in the round, first purl 1 row, then knit another 40 (44) 46 rows in stockinette stitch. Purl 1 row and then knit another 40 (44) 46 in stockinette stitch. Cast off. Fold at the purl row in the middle to the wrong side and sew in.

WELT

Pick up about 204 (220) 236 stitches along the bottom edge with the circular needle. Knitting in the round, first knit 12 rows in stockinette stitch, then purl 1 row. Knit another 12 rows in stockinette stitch. Cast off. Fold at the purl row in the middle to the wrong side and sew in.

WRISTBANDS

Pick up about 48 (56) 64 stitches with double-pointed needles. Knitting in the round, first knit 13 rows in stockinette stitch, then purl 1 row, and finally another 13 rows in stockinette stitch. Cast off. Fold at the purl row in the middle to the wrong side and sew in.

Mum's Fine One

MEASUREMENTS
(CHEST SIZE)
Small: 96cm/38 in.
(Medium: 110cm/43½ in.)
Large: 124cm/49 in.

YARN
Fingering-weight or Shetland yarn
5 (6) 7 100g balls [18 oz. (21 oz.) 24 oz.]

NEEDLES
1 pair of needles in size 2½mm (U.S.
1-2, U.K. 12-13), 1 circular needle in
size 2½mm (U.S. 1-2, U.K. 12-13) and
1 set of double-pointed needles in size
2½mm (U.S. 1-2, U.K. 12-13)

GAUGE
30 stitches to 10cm/4 in. It is
recommended to knit a gauge sample;
should your gauge differ from the one
indicated, change to smaller or larger
needles.

FRONT AND BACK
Using the circular needle, cast on 280
(320) 360 stitches. Knitting in the
round, start knitting the patterns
according to the following (see the
diagrams on the facing page):
Edge pattern: 24 (28) 32 rows.
Stockinette stitch: 8 (10) 12 rows.
Increase 8 (16) 24 stitches, distributed
at regular intervals over the first row.

Textured pattern: 24 (28) 32
horizontal repeats over 12 stitches.
Knit 13 (15) 17 vertical repeats (each
repeat consists of 10 rows).

Divide for back and front and knit
each piece separately.

Front: When a total of 20 (23) 26
repeats has been completed, slip 15
(17) 19 stitches in the middle onto a
safety pin or piece of yarn.

Knit each shoulder piece
separately and decrease for the front
neckline: 4-4-3-2-1-1 (5-4-3-2-2-1)
5-4-3-2-2-1-1-1 stitches.

Without casting off, knit until a
total of 22½ (25½) 28½ repeats has
been completed.

Do not cast off. Slip the shoulder
stitches onto a safety pin or piece of
yarn.

Back: When a total of 21½ (24½)
27½ repeats has been completed, slip
15 (17) 19 stitches in the middle
onto a safety pin or piece of yarn.

Knit each shoulder piece separately
and decrease for the back neckline:
7-4-3-1 (8-5-3-2) 9-5-3-2 stitches.

Continue knitting until the back
measures the same length as the
front, i.e., 22 ½ (25½) 28½ repeats.
From the wrong side, knit together
the shoulder stitches from the front
with those of the back, casting off at
the same time (see p. 115).

SLEEVES
Using double-pointed needles, cast
on 50 (58) 66 stitches. Knitting in the
round, start knitting the pattern
according to the following (see the
diagrams on the facing page):
Edge pattern: 24 (28) 32 rows.
Stockinette stitch: 8 (10) 12 rows.
Increase 23 (27) 31 stitches
distributed at regular intervals over
the first row.
Textured pattern: 6 (7) 8 horizontal
repeats and 1 knit stitch at the center
of the sleeve, i.e., where the sleeve
"seam" would be.

The width of the sleeve is
increased by 1 stitch at each side of
the plain stitch every 5th row.

Cast off when the sleeve measures
a total of 15 (17) 19 repeats and there
are about 133 (145) 179 stitches on
the needles.

POLO NECK
Using double-pointed needles, pick
up about 115 (130) 145 stitches.
Knitting in the round, purl 2 rows,
followed by 26 (30) 34 rows in
stockinette stitch. Purl 1 row and
then knit another 26 (30) 34 rows in
stockinette stitch. Cast off.

FINISHING
Fold the polo neck at the purl row in
the middle to the wrong side and sew
in. Sew in the sleeves.

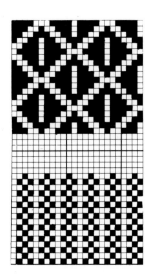

□ = knit stitch
■ = purl stitch

Textured pattern

Stockinette stitch

Edge pattern for the front and back pieces

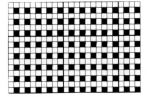

Edge pattern for the sleeves

The scarf that is seen in the photo on p. 69 is done in double stockinette stitch. This is an easy technique, which can be made all the more enjoyable by including a textured pattern with purl stitches. The sides may have different patterns, and I leave it to the reader to design a pattern of her own. Why not start knitting and let the design take shape in the process?

The scarf is knitted in a thin 2-ply woolen yarn. The gauge is 24 stitches to 10cm/4 in.

Cast on an *even* number of stitches in the usual manner. Half of these make up one side of the knitting. All rows are to be knitted in the following way: knit one, slip one with the yarn forward.

Star and Stripe

The beautiful fisherman's sweaters from Halland and Bohuslän (see pp. 25-29) were the inspiration for this sweater. My version is striped rather than checked. For a shoulder decoration I have used the delicate little floral pattern from the Ljusdal sweater (see p. 43). All the edges are done in garter stitch, but may just as well be done in ordinary ribbed knitting.

The colors of *Star* can easily be changed; however, one of the colors should be considerably lighter than the other.

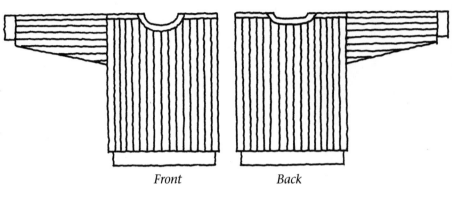

Front   *Back*

This jacket barely relates to Swedish traditional knitting, but it is done in a technique that is widely known. The texture of knitting done in this technique approximates woven material. Consequently, it is especially well suited for outdoor garments, where elasticity is not of prime importance.

Stripe, too, can easily be changed into other colors; however the contrast between the two colors has to be maintained.

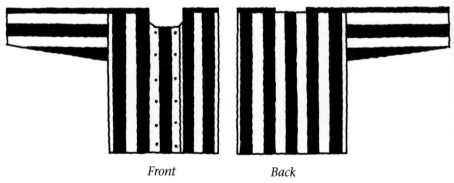

Front   *Back*

74

Star

MEASUREMENTS (CHEST SIZE)

Small: 100cm/39½ in.
(Medium: 110cm/43½ in.)
Large: 120cm/47 in.

YARN

Sport-weight yarn
Yellow: 3½ (4) 4½ 100g balls [12¼ oz.
(14 oz.) 15¾ oz.]; Red: 2½ (3) 3½
100g balls [8¾ oz. (10½ oz.) 12¼ oz.]

NEEDLES

1 circular needle in size 2½mm (U.S.
1-2, U.K. 12-13) and 3mm (U.S. 2-3,
U.K. 11), 1 pair of needles in size
3mm (U.S. 2-3, U.K. 11) and 1 set of
double-pointed needles in sizes
2½mm (U.S. 1-2, U.K. 12-13) and
3mm (U.S. 2-3, U.K. 11)

GAUGE

Garter stitch: 25 stitches to 10cm/4 in.;
two-color stockinette stitch: 30 stitches
to 10cm/4 in. It is recommended to
knit a gauge sample; should your
gauge differ from the one indicated,
change to smaller or larger needles.

FRONT AND BACK

Using the smaller circular needle and
yellow yarn, cast on 250 (280) 300
stitches.

Knitting in the round, work 27 (31)
35 rows in garter stitch, which means
purl rows alternating with knit rows.

Change to the larger circular needle
and start knitting the pattern (see the
diagram). Increase 50 (56) 60 stitches,
distributed over the first row.

Continue knitting until the work
measures 40cm/15½ in. (44cm/17½ in.)
48cm/19 in. Divide for front and back
and knit each piece separately.

When the front piece measures
16cm/6 in. (17cm/6½ in.) 19cm/7½ in.
from the division, the 11 (13) 15
middle stitches should be placed on a
safety pin or piece of yarn.

Knit each shoulder piece separately
and decrease for the front neckline:
5-3-2-1-1-1 (5-3-2-1-1-1-1) 5-4-3-2-1-1-1
stitches.

Continue knitting a few rows
without decreasing, changing from
the striped pattern to the shoulder
border according to the diagram.

Knit the shoulder border. Do not
cast off. Put the stitches on a safety
pin or piece of yarn.

Knit the back piece in the same way
up to the shoulder border. After
2 rows of the shoulder border in
yellow yarn, put the middle 23 (27)
29 stitches on a safety pin or piece of
yarn.

Knit each shoulder piece separately
and decrease for the back neckline:
3-2-1-1 (3-2-1-1) 4-3-2-1 stitches.

From the wrong side, knit the back
and front shoulder stitches together,
casting off at the same time (see p. 115).

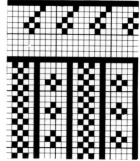

□ = yellow
■ = red

Shoulder border

Striped pattern (2 repeats)

SLEEVES

Using the smaller double-pointed
needles and yellow yarn, cast on 54
(60) 66 stitches. Knitting in the round,
work 23 (25) 27 rows in garter stitch.

Change to the larger needles and
start knitting the striped pattern,
increasing the number of stitches by
12 (18) 24 over the first row.

Increase the width of the sleeve by
2 stitches every 4 rows (1 stitch at
each side of the vertical line between
the two identical striped patterns).

Adjust the increases so that the
sleeve has a width of about 46cm/18
in. (48cm/19 in.) 54cm/21½ in. and a
length of 43cm/17 in. (47cm/18½ in.)
51cm/20 in. Cast off and sew the
sleeves onto the front and back.

NECKBAND

Pick up about 108 (116) 126 stitches
with yellow yarn and the smaller
double-pointed needles. Knitting in
the round, work 9 (11) 13 rows in
garter stitch. Cast off.

Stripe

MEASUREMENTS (CHEST SIZE)
Small: 102cm/40 in.
(Medium: 110cm/43½ in.)
Large: 118cm/46½ in.

YARN
Fingering-weight or Shetland yarn
Yellow and red: 3 (3½) 4 100g balls of
each color [10½ oz. (12¼ oz.) 14 oz.]

NEEDLES
1 pair size 4mm (U.S. 5-6, U.K. 8)

GAUGE
30 stitches to 10cm/4 in. It is
recommended to knit a gauge
sample; should your gauge differ
from the one indicated, change to
smaller or larger needles.

The jacket is knitted from side
seam to side seam. The technique is
identical with that used in *Ticking*
(see p. 83), but in *Stripe* the wrong
side will actually function as the
front (right) side.

KNITTING TECHNIQUE
Row 1: *Knit 1, slip 1 with yarn
forward.*
Row 2: *Purl 1, slip 1 with yarn back.*

LEFT FRONT
Using yellow yarn, cast on 158 (170)
182 stitches. Knit 16 (18) 20 rows,
making edge stitches on both sides.

Edge stitch: The first stitch of every
row is knitted (plain) from the back
loop. The last stitch of every row is
slipped as if it had been purled, with
the yarn forward.

Change to red yarn and knit 26
(28) 30 rows.

Change to yellow yarn and knit 16
(18) 20 rows. Increase 1 stitch inside
the edge stitch on the left side every
second row 4 times.

Change to red yarn, make another
2 increases and then cast on 12 (16)
20 stitches on the same side as the
increases. In all, knit 26 (28) 30 rows
in red.

Change to yellow and knit 24 (26)
28 rows.

Change to red and knit 26 (28) 30
rows.

Change to yellow and knit 14 (16)
18 rows. Cast off.

RIGHT FRONT
Knit the right front like the left front
piece, but reverse the patterning and
shaping.

Buttonholes should be made after
the first 7 (8) 9 yellow rows. Starting
from the right, knit the edge stitch
and another 4 stitches. Cast off 3
stitches for the buttonhole, knit

25 (27) 29 stitches, cast off 3, knit 25
(27) 29, cast off 3, etc., until 6
buttonholes have been made.

In the following row, 3 stitches are
cast on in the places where the
casting off was done.

BACK
Using yellow yarn, cast on 176 (192)
208 stitches. Knit a straight piece
with edge stitches at either end. First
knit 14 (16) 18 rows in yellow.
Change to red yarn. The red stripes
have 26 (28) 30 rows, whereas the
yellow have 24 (26) 28 rows. Knit
red and yellow stripes alternately
until there are 5 red and 4 yellow
stripes. Finish off with 14 (16) 18
rows in yellow.

SLEEVES
The sleeve is knitted from side seam to
side seam. Using yellow yarn, cast on
128 (140) 152 stitches. Knit 4 rows.

Knit edge stitches at either end.

Change to red yarn and knit 2
rows over 7 stitches followed by 2
rows over 14, 2 rows over 21, 2 rows
over 28, 2 rows over 36, etc., with an
increase of 8 working stitches every
other row. Change to yellow yarn
after 26 (28) 30 rows of red and knit
24 (26) 28 rows.

Change to red yarn and knit 26 (28) 30 rows.

Change to yellow and knit 24 (26) 28 rows.

Change to red yarn and cast on 52 (58) 64 stitches at the wide side of the sleeve. Knit 26 (28) 30 rows. Cast off the additional 52 (58) 64 stitches.

Change to yellow yarn and after 24 (26) 28 rows to red. Knit 26 (28) 30 rows in red.

Change to yellow yarn and after the same number of rows as after the last increase on the other side, the number of working stitches is reduced by 8 every second row.

Change to red yarn after 24 (26) 28 rows of yellow.

When there are 28 stitches left on the needle, start decreasing by 7 every other row.

Knit 4 rows in yellow yarn over all the stitches. Cast off.

FINISHING

Join the lengthened red stripes of the sleeves with the shoulders of the back and front pieces.

Finish sewing the sleeves to the back and front.

Join the side seams.

As the photo on p. 75 shows, the front pieces overlap. Sew buttons onto the left front piece.

Sew on buttons in the middle of the yellow stripe on the right front piece to create the impression of a double-breasted jacket.

Jolly and Ticking

Jolly is knitted in two-color stockinette stitch, in a pattern that is clearly influenced by the knitted sleeve from Gagnef (see p. 33). Its edges, done in stockinette stitch, curl a little, and the armhole gussets are both decorative and functional since they increase the sleeve width (which is otherwise quite small). The distances between the patterns are so large that the yarn will have to be knitted into or sewn onto the main-color knitting when the sweater is completed. The latter method is preferable, as it can be done with the same color as the main knitting.

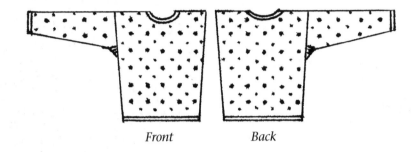

Front   *Back*

Ticking is not inspired by traditional knitting, but is knitted in an interesting, yet widely used, technique. The texture approximates woven material, which makes the garment suitable for outdoor wear.

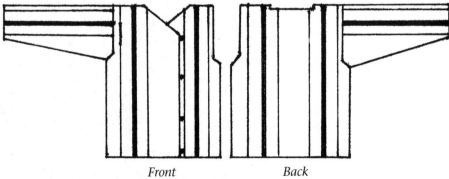

Front   *Back*

Jolly

MEASUREMENTS (CHEST SIZE)
Small: 92cm/36 in.
(Medium: 107cm/42 in.)
Large: 122cm/48 in.

YARN
Fingering-weight or Shetland yarn
Red: 4½ (5) 5½ 100g balls [15¾ oz.
(17¾ oz.) 19½ oz.]; Green: ½ (½) ½
100g ball [1¾ oz. (1¾ oz.) 1¾ oz.]

NEEDLES
1 circular needle in size 2½mm (U.S.
1-2, U.K. 12-13) and 1 pair double-
pointed needles in size 2½mm (U.S.
1-2, U.K. 12-13)

GAUGE
30 stitches to 10cm/4 in. It is
recommended to knit a gauge
sample; should your gauge differ
from the one indicated, change to
smaller or larger needles.

FRONT AND BACK
Using red yarn and the circular
needle, cast on 254 (286) 318 stitches.
    Knitting in the round, knit 8 rows
of stockinette stitch, followed by
1 purl row.
    Knit another 12 (14) 16 rows in
stockinette stitch.
    Start knitting the pattern
according to the diagram and
increase 1 stitch on each side of the
"seams." Repeat the increase about
every 14 rows.
    After knitting 3 complete pattern
repeats and 1 additional pattern
shape, divide for front and back in the
middle of the "seams."
    Knit the front piece on the pair of
needles. After about 56 (64) 78 rows,
put the 13 (15) 17 stitches in the
middle on a safety pin or piece of
yarn.
    Knit each side separately and cast
off for the front neckline every other
row: 5-4-3-2-1-1 (5-4-3-2-1-1-1-1)
5-4-3-2-1-1-1-1-1 stitches.
    Continue knitting without
decreasing another 8 (10) 12 rows,
followed by 1 purl row on the right
side and 1 purl row on the wrong
(purl) side. Do not cast off, but place
the stitches on a safety pin or piece of
yarn.
    Knit 2 complete pattern repeats and
7 (9) 11 rows of the back piece; then
put the middle 15 (17) 19 stitches on a
safety pin or piece of yarn.
    Knit each side separately and cast
off every other row 9-3-2-1 (10-4-2-1)
11-4-2-1. Make sure that the number
of shoulder stitches is the same as that
on the front piece. As was done in
knitting the front piece, knit a purl
row on the right side, followed by a
purl row on the wrong side. Put the
stitches on a safety pin or piece of yarn.

SLEEVES
Using red yarn and double-pointed
needles, cast on 66 (73) 80 stitches.
    Knitting in the round, knit 8 rows
in stockinette stitch, followed by 1
purl row.
    Knit another 12 (14) 16 rows in
stockinette stitch.
    Start knitting the pattern according
to the diagram and increase 1 stitch
at each side of the "seam." Repeat
this increase every 8 rows.
    When the sleeve measures about
42cm/16½ in. (46cm/18 in.)
50cm/19½ in., there should be about
114 (127) 144 stitches on the needles.
    Cast off, except for the 24 (28) 32
stitches around the "seam." Knit
these in garter stitch, casting off
1 stitch at each side at the beginning
of each row until there are no more
stitches. The armhole gusset is now
completed.

NECKBAND
Transfer the shoulder stitches onto
needles. Put the back and front
pieces together, the right sides
toward each other. Knit together 1
stitch from the back with 1 from the
front, casting off at the same time.
    Using the double-pointed needles,
pick up about 100 (118) 136 stitches.
Knitting in the round, purl the first
row and then knit 10 (10) 12 rows in
stockinette stitch. Cast off.

DIAGRAM FOR THE FRONT

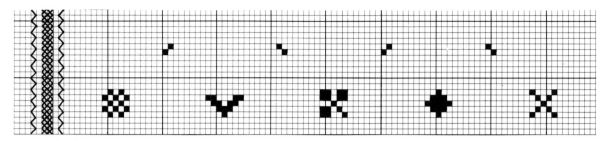

DIAGRAM FOR THE BACK

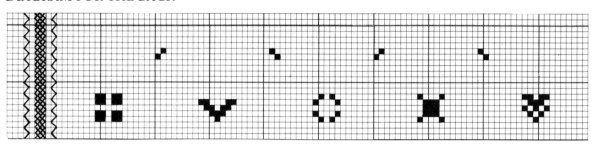

DIAGRAM FOR THE LEFT SLEEVE

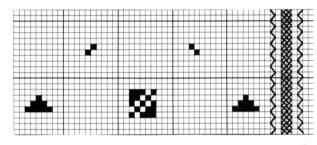

DIAGRAM FOR THE RIGHT SLEEVE

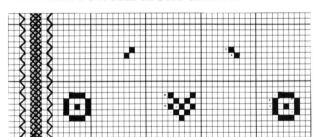

NUMBER OF STITCHES AND ROWS BETWEEN THE PATTERN SHAPES
22 sts/32 rows (26 sts/36 rows) 28 sts/40 rows

□ = red
■ = green
✕ = purl stitch
> = increases

FINISHING
Join the sleeves to the front and
back. One side of the armhole gusset
is sewn onto the front, the other
onto the back.

82

Ticking

MEASUREMENTS
(CHEST SIZE)
Small: 110cm/43½ in.
(Medium: 120cm/47 in.)
Large: 130cm/51 in.

YARN
Fingering-weight or Shetland yarn
Black: 4½ (5) 6 100g balls [15¾ oz.
(17¾ oz.) 21 oz.]; Red: 3½ (4) 5 100g
balls [12¼ oz. (14 oz.) 17¾ oz.];
Green: ½ (1) 1 100g ball [1¾ oz.
(3½ oz.) 3½ oz.]

NEEDLES
1 pair in size 4mm (U.S. 5-6, U.K. 8)

GAUGE
28 stitches to 10cm/4 in. It is
recommended to knit a gauge
sample; should your gauge differ
from the one indicated, change to
smaller or larger needles.

KNITTING TECHNIQUE
The number of stitches has to be even.
Row 1: (Wrong side) *purl 1, slip 1
with yarn back.*
Row 2: *Knit 1, slip 1 with yarn
forward.*

FRONTS
This piece is knitted from front edge
to side seam.

Using black yarn, cast on 144 (160)
170 stitches.

On the left side, knit an edge
stitch. The last stitch is slipped with
the yarn forward; the first stitch is
knitted from the back loop of the
stitch.

On the right side, increase 1 stitch
every second row inside 1 edge stitch,
which is knitted on the left side.

After 56 (60) 64 rows, change to
red yarn. Continue the increases
another 4 (6) 8 times, i.e., 8 (12) 16
rows.

Knit a total of 20 (24) 28 rows
with red yarn.

Change to green. Knit 6 (8) 10
rows.

Change to red. Knit 20 (24) 28
rows.

Change to black. Knit 28 (30) 32
rows.

Cast off 64 (70) 76 stitches for the
armhole. Knit 16 (20) 24 black rows.
Cast off.

The second front piece is knitted
in the same way, but with reversed
patterning and shaping.

BACK
This piece is knitted from side seam
to side seam.

Using black yarn, cast on 112 (126)
134 stitches.

On one side (the lower edge of the
jacket), an edge stitch is knitted. Knit
16 (20) 24 rows.

Cast on 64 (70) 76 stitches for the
armhole on the side without an edge
stitch.

Knit 28 (30) 32 rows.

Change to red. Knit 20 (24) 28
rows.

Change to green. Knit 6 (8) 10
rows.

Change to red. Knit 12 rows.

Decrease 4 (6) 8 stitches (2 stitches
are knitted together every other row
inside the first stitch).

The red section should consist of
20 (24) 28 rows.

Change to black. Knit 56 (60) 64
rows.

Change to red. Increase 1 stitch
every second row inside the first
stitch, i.e., 4 (6) 8 stitches and 8 (12)
16 rows. Knit another 12 rows in red
yarn.

Change to green. Knit 6 (8) 10
rows.

Change to red. Knit 20 (24) 28
rows.

Change to black. Knit 28 (30) 32
rows.

Cast off 64 (70) 76 stitches. Knit
another 16 (20) 24 rows.

Cast off.

SLEEVES

This piece is knitted from side seam to side seam. Using black yarn, cast on 8 (10) 12 stitches. Knit 2 rows. Then start increasing, on one side, 8 stitches every second row. When there are 118 (128) 140 stitches on the needle, knit another 8 (12) 16 rows with black yarn.

Change to red. Knit 20 (24) 28 rows.

Change to green. Knit 6 (8) 10 rows.

Change to red. Knit 20 (24) 28 rows.

Change to black. Knit 36 (40) 44 rows.

Change to red. Knit 20 (24) 28 rows.

Change to green. Knit 6 (8) 10 rows.

Change to red. Knit 20 (24) 28 rows.

Change to black. Knit 8 (12) 16 rows. Then start decreasing 8 stitches every second row on one side. Knit a total of 38 (42) 46 rows with black yarn, after which there should be 8 (10) 12 stitches on the needle. Cast off.

The other sleeve is knitted in the same way.

FINISHING

Join the side and shoulder seams. Make sure that the stripes match at the shoulder. Join the sleeve seams. Join the sleeves to the front and back.

On the right front piece, crochet 4 loops to be used as buttonholes. Sew on buttons to the left front piece.

Quadrille and Chess Jacket

Quadrille is an adaptation of patterns found in the Delsbo and Bjuråker sweaters described on pp. 51-55. However, the patterns are created not by multicolored knitting, but by using textured knitting, i.e., purl stitches on a plain stockinette background, which is a characteristic of the Scanian *spede* sweaters.

The front and back pieces feature different patterns. The upper edge of the back has a green, white and red border pattern; otherwise it has the same textured pattern as the sleeves.

Chess Jacket is knitted very tightly, so it is suitable for outdoor use. The black squares are knitted with cotton yarn (8/4), and the red with 2-ply woolen yarn. This feels comfortable. The idea of trying out this combination stems from the Hälsingland sweaters, where the white parts were often knitted with cotton yarn.

It is easy change the colors of *Chess Jacket;* however, one color should be darker than the other.

Quadrille

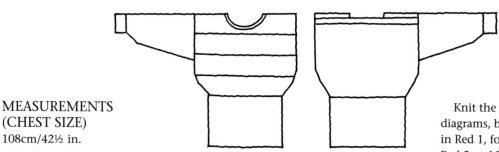

Front   *Back*

MEASUREMENTS
(CHEST SIZE)
108cm/42½ in.

YARN
Sport-weight yarn
Black: 1½ 100g balls [5¼ oz.]; Green:
a very small quantity; Red 1
(yellowish, saturated): 4 100g balls [14
oz.]; Red 2 (ordinary red): ½ 100g ball
[1¾ oz.]; Red 3 (orange red): ½ 100g
ball [1¾ oz.]; Red 4 (cherry red): ¼
100g ball [1 oz.]; Natural white: a very
small quantity.

NEEDLES
1 circular needle in size 2mm (U.S. 0,
U.K. 14), 1 set of double-pointed
needles in sizes 2mm (U.S. 0, U.K. 14)
and 2½mm (U.S. 1-2, U.K. 12-13) and
1 pair of 2½mm needles (U.S. 1-2,
U.K. 12-13)

GAUGE
Ribbing: 30 stitches to 10cm/4 in.;
textured pattern: 26 stitches to
10cm/4 in. It is recommended to knit
a gauge sample; should your gauge
differ from the one indicated, change
to smaller or larger needles.

FRONT AND BACK
Using black yarn and a circular
needle, cast on 266 stitches. Knit the
ribbing according to the diagram,

distributed in the following way:
9 purl stitches at each side of the
garment and between these, 14
pattern repeats minus 2 purl stitches.

Knit 26 4-row vertical pattern repeats.

Change to green yarn and knit 1
row and purl 1 row.

The rest of the body piece is
knitted in four parts: front and back
pieces and garter-stitch "seam
ribbons" between them.

The ribbons are a continuation of
the 9 purled side stitches in the
ribbing and should be knitted in Red 4
garter stitch on the pair of ordinary
needles. However, the 9 stitches should
be increased to 14 over the first row.

Continue knitting the ribbons until
they measure about 20cm/8 in., or
about 106 rows. Cast off.

The front is knitted in Red 1 yarn on
the pair of needles. Increase the number
of stitches over the first row from 124 to
135, i.e., by 11 stitches, two of which
make up the edge stitches.

Diagram for ribbing

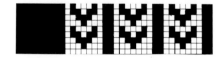

Knit the pattern according to the
diagrams, beginning with Diagram 1
in Red 1, followed by Diagram 2 in
Red 2 and Diagram 1 in Red 3.
Between each diagrams and after the
last diagram, 2 rows should be knitted
in green: 1 knit row and 1 purl row
(from the right side).

Put the 13 center stitches on a spare
needle.

Knit each shoulder piece separately
in stockinette stitch, using Red 1.
Continue shaping the neckline by
decreasing 4-4-3-2-1-1. Knit 26
shoulder rows in stockinette stitch
without shaping. Cast off the
shoulder stitches.

The back is knitted in Red 1 on the
pair of needles.

Increase the number of stitches
over the first row from 124 to 131,
i.e., by 7 stitches, 2 of which make up
the edge stitches.

Knit the pattern according to the
diagrams.

After 8½ repeats and 1 row, change
to green yarn and knit the upper edge
border pattern according to the
diagram. The actual pattern begins
after the first 4 stitches.

Cast off 46 stitches at each shoulder
side and knit another 10 rows in
stockinette stitch over the 39 center
stitches. This piece will be folded and
sewn on to the wrong side.

DIAGRAM FRONT

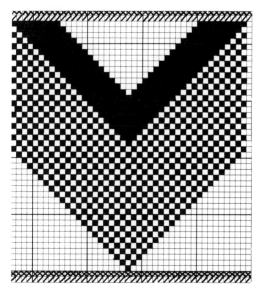

Diagram 1.

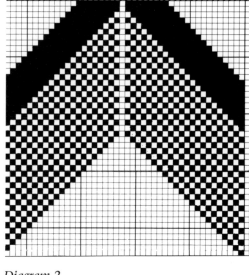

Diagram 2.

SLEEVES

Using the smaller double-pointed needles and Red 1 yarn, cast on 56 stitches.

Knit the ribbing according to the diagram: 6 repeats of 9 stitches plus 2 purl stitches. The additional stitches form a seam-like stripe under the arm. Knit 5 4-row vertical repeats.

Change to the larger double-pointed needles and increase 6 stitches over the first row.

Knit the pattern according to the diagram. The center of a pattern shape is the center of the sleeve. The 4 purl stitches, i.e., the "seam" of the cuff, should be knitted in garter stitch.

Increase 1 stitch at each side of these stitches every 6th row.

Knit 9 pattern repeats plus 5 rows into the following one.

Increase 1 stitch every second row 4 times at each end of the 4 seam stitches. Knit 2 rows in stockinette stitch, but

continue the garter stitches in the seam. There should now be about 130 stitches on the needle.

Purl every other row 5 times.

Cast off the sleeve stitches.

An alternate way to knit the sleeve is to pick up stitches at the armhole and knit from top to bottom.

FINISHING

Join the pieces at the shoulders. Join the seam ribbons with the front and back.

Sew in the sleeves. Join the garter-stitch sleeve seams with the ribbons of the front and back.

NECKBAND

Using the pair of needles and Red 4 yarn, pick up about 80 stitches along the front neckline.

Knit the first row (purl on the right side), followed by 1 knit row and 1 purl row. Cast off. Join the Red 4 edges with the back.

 = knit stitch
■ = purl stitch
/ = green knit stitch
× = green purl row
● = natural white
◢ = Red 3

Diagram for back, sleeves and upper edge border of the back

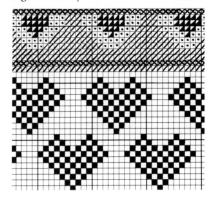

Chess Jacket

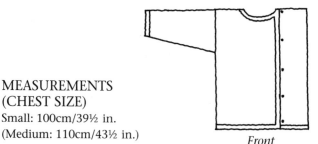

Front   *Back*

MEASUREMENTS (CHEST SIZE)

Small: 100cm/39½ in.
(Medium: 110cm/43½ in.)
Large: 120cm/47 in.

YARN

Fingering-weight or Shetland red yarn: 5 (5½) 6 100g balls [17¾ oz. (19½ oz.) 21 oz.]; Black cotton yarn 8/4: 5 (5½) 6 100g balls [17¾ oz. (19½ oz.) 21 oz.]

NEEDLES

1 circular needle in sizes 2½mm (U.S. 1-2, U.K. 12-13) and 3mm (U.S. 2-3, U.K. 11), 1 set of double-pointed needles sizes 2½mm (U.S. 1-2, U.K. 12-13) and 3mm (U.S. 2-3, U.K. 11) and 1 pair of needles size 3mm (U.S. 2-3, U.K. 11)

GAUGE

32 stitches to 10cm/4 in. It is recommended to knit a gauge sample; should your gauge differ from the one indicated, change to smaller or larger needles.

FRONT AND BACK

Using the smaller circular needle and red yarn, cast on 400 (432) 464 stitches.

Knit 7 rows in garter stitch back and forth, i.e., not in the round. Slip the edge stitch if it is the last stitch or knit it through the back of the stitch if it is the first. Put 8 stitches at each end on safety pins. Change to the larger circular needle, and knit in

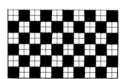

Pattern diagram

the round, but cast on 8 stitches (for the front seam, which will be cut after the knitting has been completed). Knit the pattern according to the diagram above.

When the work measures 38cm/15 in. (40cm/15½ in.) 42cm/16½ in., the front and back pieces should be knitted separately. The front consists of 224 (240) 256 stitches; the back of 168 (184) 200 stitches. When front measures 53cm/21 in. (54cm/21½ in.) 56cm/22 in., knit 76 (80) 84 stitches, put the following 14 (16) 18 stitches on a spare needle or

safety pin, knit 44 (48) 52 stitches, purl 14 (16) 18 stitches on a spare needle, knit 76 (80) 84 stitches.

Continue shaping the neckline at each side of the stitches that have been put on spare needles, by decreasing: 4-3-3-3-2-2-1 (4-3-3-3-2-2-2-1) 4-3-3-3-3-2-2-1-1 stitches. 8 center stitches should now remain between the neck shapings. Cast these off.

Knit each shoulder piece separately for about another 8 (12) 14 rows, the last row ending in the middle of a pattern square. Put the shoulder stitches on a spare needle or safety pin.

Knit the back until it measures about 56cm/22 in. (60cm/23½ in.) 64cm/25 in. Put the 38 (40) 44 center stitches on a spare needle. (4½ squares now remain to be knitted up to the shoulder. Make sure that the number of vertical squares are the same for front and back.)

Knit each shoulder piece separately and continue shaping the neckline by decreasing: 2-2-1-1 (3-2-2-1) 3-3-2-1 stitches.

Knit the shoulder stitches together, casting off at the same time (see p. 115). Black should be knitted together with black, and red with red.

88

SLEEVES

Using the larger double-pointed needles, pick up about 155 (161) 177 stitches at the armhole. Knit the pattern according to the diagram. Keep knitting the center stitch under the arm ("sleeve seam") in red, decreasing 1 stitch at each side of it every 7th row.

Change to the smaller double-pointed needles when the sleeve measures 42cm/16½ in. (44cm/17½ in.) 48cm/19 in. Knit 1 row and purl 1 row 4 times. Cast off.

FINISHING

Mark the position of mid-front by tacking stitches. Using a sewing machine, zigzag twice at each side of the tacking. Cut between the zigzag seams.

FRONT BANDS

Put the 8 stitches from the safety pin onto the pair of needles and knit in garter stitch, making an edge stitch at the outer side.

Knit the band until it measures the same length as the front piece; then decrease 1 stitch every other row at the side without an edge stitch until no stitch remains.

Sew the band onto the front (on top and overlapping), working from the right side, using invisible stitches.

Fold the seam edges of the front piece and sew them to the wrong side.

NECKBAND

Using the smaller circular needle and red yarn, pick up about 180 (190) 200 stitches from the top of one front band, over the neck shapings of the front and back to the top of the other front band.

Using circular needle, knit back and forth in garter stitch for 10 rows. Cast off.

BUTTONS AND BUTTONHOLES

Crochet 4 to 5 loops on the right front band to be used as buttonholes. Sew on buttons to the left front piece.

Lassie and Curlicue

The Gotland sweater on p. 31 is the source of inspiration for *Lassie*. The combination of fisherman's rib and garter stitch aroused my interest. However, I adapted the original pattern a little, knitting this sweater in two colors and with garter-stitch edges. The garter-stitch waistband is buttoned at the side, with a tiny zigzag eyelet border just like the front pieces of the *källingtröja*.

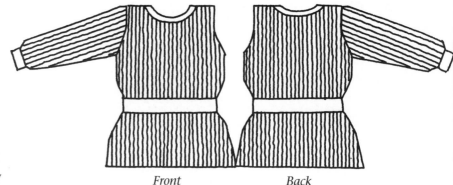

Front　　　　　*Back*

Curlicue, as shown and described here, is a straight long slipover. Needless to say, it can easily be made shorter by reducing the number of vertical pattern repeats.

The pattern is not really related to any of the historical garments in Part I, but has been designed independently.

The colors may very well be changed; however, it is recommended that the two pattern colors contrast with the main color and that one of them be darker and the other brighter.

Front　　　　　*Back*

Lassie

MEASUREMENTS
(CHEST SIZE)
Small: 90cm/35½ in.
(Medium: 100cm/39½ in.)
Length: 62cm/24½in. (68cm/27 in.)

YARN
Sport-weight yarn
Red: 3½ (4) 100g balls [12¼ oz.
(14 oz.)]; Blue: 3 (3) 100g balls [10½ oz.
(10½ oz.)]

NEEDLES
1 set long double-pointed needles or
circular needle in size 2½mm (U.S.
1-2, U.K. 12-13) and 1 set short
double-pointed needles in size 2½mm
(U.S. 1-2, U.K. 12-13)

GAUGE
Garter stitch: 27 stitches to 10cm/4 in.;
fisherman's rib: 22 stitches to 10cm/4 in.
It is recommended to knit a gauge
sample; should your gauge differ from
the one indicated, change to smaller
or larger needles.

PATTERN
Fisherman's rib in two colors.
Multiple of 2.
Row 1: (Wrong side) (Red yarn) 1 edge
stitch, *1 yarn round needle (yrn), slip
1, purl 1,* 1 edge stitch.
   Do not turn the knitting after the
row has been completed, i.e., start

row 2 on the same side as row 1.
Row 2: (blue yarn) 1 edge stitch,
*knit together the slipped stitch and
the yrn from the preceding row, 1
yrn, slip 1,* 1 edge stitch.
   Turn the knitting.
Row 3: (red yarn) 1 edge stitch, *knit
together the yrn and the slipped
stitch, 1 yrn, slip 1,* 1 edge stitch.
   Do not turn the knitting.
Row 4: (blue yarn) 1 edge stitch, *1
yrn, slip 1, purl together the yrn and
the slipped stitch,* 1 edge stitch.
   Turn the knitting.
Row 5: (red yarn) 1 edge stitch, *1
yrn, slip 1, purl together the slipped
stitch and the yrn,* 1 edge stitch.
   Do not turn the knitting.
Row 6: (blue yarn) 1 edge stitch,
*knit together the yrn and the
slipped stitch, 1 yrn, slip 1,* 1 edge
stitch.
   Turn the knitting.
   Repeat rows 3-6.

FRONT
Cast on 108 (120) stitches plus 2
edge stitches.
   Knit two-color fisherman's rib
according to the above pattern until
work measures 22cm/8½ in.
(25cm/10 in.).
   Change to garter stitch in red
yarn, casting on 6 stitches at the
right side for button band and

decreasing 8 stitches over the rest of
the row.
   Knit 36 rows in garter stitch, with
the eyelet pattern to the right,
starting from the front side.

Eyelet pattern:
Row 1: 1 edge stitch, K4, K2 tog., 1 yrn.
Row 2 and all even rows: Knit.
Row 3: 1 edge stitch, K3, K2 tog., 1
yrn, K1.
Row 5: 1 edge stitch, K2, K2 tog., 1
yrn, K2.
Row 7: 1 edge stitch, K1, K2 tog., 1
yrn, K2.
Row 9: 1 edge stitch, K2 tog., 1 yrn,
K4.
Row 11: 1 edge stitch, K2, 1 yrn, K2
tog., K2
Row 13: 1 edge stitch, K3, 1 yrn, K2
tog., K1.
Row 15: 1 edge stitch, K4, 1 yrn, K2
tog.
Repeat rows 1-16, ending with row 1.
   Cast off the 6 stitches of the
button band.
   Change to two-color fisherman's
rib according to pattern, beginning
with Row 1 from the wrong side, and
knit 17cm/6½ in. (18cm/7 in.). Cast
off for the armhole shaping: 7-2-2-1
(8-3-2-1) stitches.
   Please note that "yarn round
needle" (yrn) does not count as a
stitch when decreasing or increasing.

When the fisherman's rib measures 30cm/12 in. (31cm/12 in.) from the waistline, cast off the 7 center stitches for the neckline.

Each shoulder piece is knitted separately. Continue decreasing for the neckline: 4-3-2-1-1 (5-3-2-2-1) stitches. Knit 10 rows without shaping. Cast off.

BACK

Knit as for the front, but increase the number of stitches at the left side when changing to garter stitch at the waistline, and do not knit the eyelet pattern.

When the fisherman's rib measures 31cm/12 in. (32cm/12½ in.) from the waistline, cast off the 17 (21) center stitches for the neckline.

The shoulder pieces are knitted separately. Continue decreasing for the neckline: 3-2-1 (3-2-1) stitches, followed by 6 rows without shaping. Cast off.

SLEEVES

Using red yarn, cast on 57 (61) stitches plus 2 edge stitches. Knit 24 (28) rows in garter stitch.

Change to fisherman's rib, starting from the wrong side.

Increase 1 stitch at each end inside the edge stitches every 5cm/2 in. In all, 6 to 7 stitches should be added at each side.

When the sleeve measures 33cm/13 in. (35cm/15 in.), cast off at each side every other row: 3-3-2 (4-3-2) stitches, 1 stitch 10 (11) times, 2-3-4-4 (2-3-4-5) stitches.

Cast off the remaining stitches.

FINISHING

Join the shoulder and side seams, except for the piece by the waistline where the buttons are. Sew two buttons onto the side without the eyelet pattern.

Join the sleeve seams. Fit them into the armholes and sew in.

NECKBAND

Using short double-pointed needles and red yarn, pick up about 120 (130) stitches.

Knit garter stitch in the round (purl and knit rows alternately) for 13 rows. Cast off.

Curlicue

MEASUREMENTS (CHEST SIZE)
Small: 96cm/38 in.
(Medium: 108cm/42½ in.)
Large: 120cm/47 in.

NUMBER OF PATTERN REPEATS
16 (18) 20

YARN
Sport-weight yarn
Red: 3 (4) 5 100g balls [10½ oz. (14 oz.) 17¾ oz.]; Dark blue: 1 (1) 1 100g ball [3½ oz. (3½ oz.) 3½ oz.]; Bright blue: ¼ (¼) ¼ 100g ball [1 oz. (1 oz.) 1 oz.]

NEEDLES
1 circular needle in sizes 2½mm (U.S. 1-2, U.K. 12-13) and 3mm (U.S. 2-3, U.K. 11), 1 pair of needles in size 3mm (U.S. 2-3, U.K. 11) and 1 set of double-pointed needles in size 2½mm (U.S. 1-2, U.K. 12-13)

GAUGE
Garter stitch: 27 stitches to 10cm/4 in.; two-color stockinette stitch: 27 stitches to 10cm/4 in. It is recommended to knit a gauge sample; should your gauge differ from the one indicated, change to smaller or larger needles.

PATTERN DIAGRAM

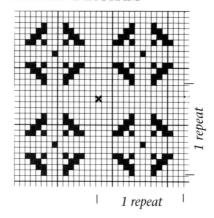

1 repeat (vertical)

1 repeat (horizontal)

□ = red
■ = dark blue
✕ = bright blue

FRONT AND BACK
Using the smaller circular needle and red yarn, cast on 240 (270) 300 stitches.

Knit 15 (15) 17 rows in garter stitch (when knitting in the round this means purling every other row and knitting every other row).

Change to stockinette stitch and increase by 16 (18) 20 stitches over the first row. Knit 6 rows.

Change to the larger circular needle and knit the pattern according to the diagram.

When work measures 11 (12) 13 vertical pattern repeats, divide for front and back and knit each piece separately, starting with the front.

Start casting off for the armhole at the bright blue stitch: 10 (10) 10 and continue casting off 3-3-2-1-1-1 (3-3-3-2-1-1-1) 4-3-3-2-2-1-1-1 stitches.

Continue knitting without shaping until the front measures 14 (15) 16 vertical pattern repeats. Put the 13 (15) 17 center stitches onto a spare needle or piece of yarn.

Knit each shoulder piece separately and continue shaping the front neckline by casting off:

5-3-2-1-1-1 (6-3-2-1-1-1-1-1) 6-4-3-2-1-1-1-1 stitches.

All in all, knit 1½ (1½) 2 pattern repeats from the beginning of the neckline.

Purl 1 row from the right side and 1 row from the wrong side. Put the shoulder stitches on a spare needle or piece of yarn.

Knit the back, casting off for the armhole as follows: 7-3-3-2-1-1-1 (7-3-3-2-2-1-1-1-1) 7-4-3-3-2-2-1-1-1 stitches.

Continue knitting without shaping until the back measures 16 vertical pattern repeats. Put the 25 (29) 33 center stitches onto a spare needle or piece of yarn.

Knit each shoulder piece separately and continue casting off for the back neckline: 4-2-1 (5-3-1) 5-3-2-1 stitches.

Make sure that the number of shoulder stitches is the same for front and back.

Add half of a pattern repeat for size Large.

Conclude by purling 1 row from the right side and 1 row from the wrong side.

Knit the shoulder stitches together, casting off at the same time (see p. 115).

NECKBAND

Using double-pointed needles and red yarn, pick up about 100 (116) 136 stitches.

Knit 12 (12) 14 rows in garter stitch. Cast off.

ARMHOLE BANDS

Using double-pointed needles and red yarn, pick up about 130 (140) 154 stitches. Knit as for neckband.

Potpourri

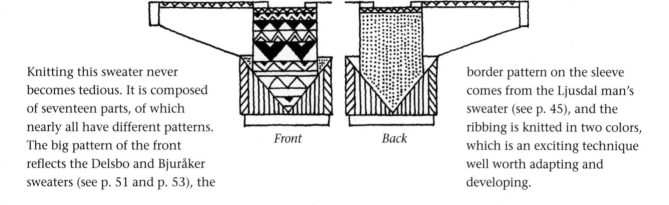

Front   *Back*

Knitting this sweater never becomes tedious. It is composed of seventeen parts, of which nearly all have different patterns. The big pattern of the front reflects the Delsbo and Bjuråker sweaters (see p. 51 and p. 53), the border pattern on the sleeve comes from the Ljusdal man's sweater (see p. 45), and the ribbing is knitted in two colors, which is an exciting technique well worth adapting and developing.

MEASUREMENTS (CHEST SIZE)
118cm/46½ in.

YARN
Sport-weight yarn
Brick red: 4 100g balls [14 oz.]; Dark blue: 4 100g balls [14 oz.] Wine colored: 1½ 100g balls [5¼ oz.]; Turquoise: 1 100g ball [3½ oz.]

NEEDLES
1 circular needle in size 3½mm (U.S. 4, U.K. 9-10), 1 set of double-pointed needles in size 3½mm (U.S. 4, U.K. 9-10), 1 pair of needles in size 4mm (U.S. 5-6, U.K. 8) and 1 crochet hook 3½mm (U.S. E/4, U.K. G)

GAUGE
24 stitches to 10cm/4 in. It is recommended to knit a gauge sample; should your gauge differ from the one indicated, change to smaller or larger needles.

Cast on and knit the various sections of the sweater according to the diagrams on pp. 98-99. (The lower edge and the cuffs are knitted onto the completed sweater at the end.)

Join the parts making up the front and back. The sleeve sections are crocheted together from the right side with dark blue yarn. The sleeve is crocheted onto the front and back in the same way.

For the lower edge (the welt), pick up 266 stitches using the circular needle and brick-red yarn. Knit according to the diagram.

For the cuff, pick up 56 stitches using double-pointed needles and brick-red yarn. Knit according to the diagram.

Make two braids from double brick-red yarn. The braid should begin at the upper and outer points of the small triangle. The braid covers the seams of the back and front and is sewn onto these.

Diagram 1. The back has the same shape and number of stitches as the front, but the pattern is simpler.

Diagram 3. For the back, the corresponding pieces are knitted in plain turquoise.

Diagram 1.

Diagram 2 (right). Note that the straight edge farthest to the right constitutes the center; the pattern is reversed on the back.

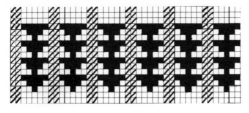

Diagram 7.

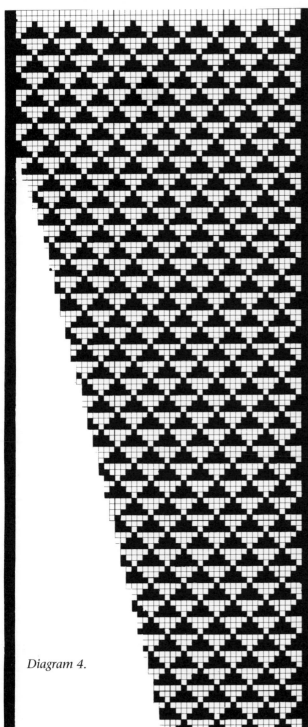

Diagram 4.

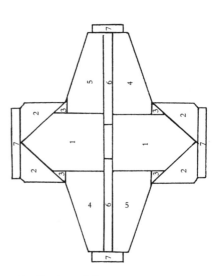

Diagram 6.

□ = *brick red*
■ = *dark blue*
● = *wine*
× = *turquoise*
/ = *purl stitch*

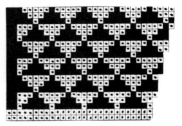

Distribution of diagrams

Diagram 5.

Mirror

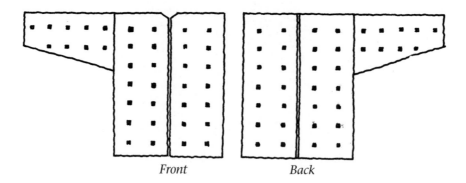

Front   Back

A plain and simple jacket that
goes as well with a skirt as with a
pair of trousers. The pattern is
inspired by knitting techniques as
found in the Scanian *spede*
sweaters, where purl stitches form
a textured pattern on a
stockinette-stitch background.
However, in *Mirror* the pattern is
reversed in that the little square is
knitted in stockinette stitch,
whereas the background is done
in garter stitch. At the center of
the back, side seams and sleeve
seams the jacket features
stockinette-stitch stripes, made up
of stitches that have been slipped
every other row.

Mirror

MEASUREMENTS (CHEST SIZE)
Small: 100cm/39½ in.
(Medium: 120cm/47 in.)
Large: 130cm/51 in.

YARN
Double-knitting-weight yarn
8 (9) 10 100g balls [28 oz. (31 oz.)
35 oz.]

NEEDLES
1 set in size 3½mm (U.S. 4, U.K. 9-10)

GAUGE
22 stitches to 10cm/4 in. It is
recommended to knit a gauge
sample; should your gauge differ
from the one indicated, change to
smaller or larger needles.

FRONTS
Cast on 59 (65) 71 stitches.

Knit 26 rows in garter stitch,
knitting an edge stitch at the right-
hand side, i.e., the last stitch is
slipped with the yarn forward, the
first stitch is knitted through the back.

At the left-hand side, slip 3 stitches
every other row, i.e., with the wrong
side facing, with the yarn forward.

Knit the pattern according to the
diagram.

PATTERN DIAGRAM

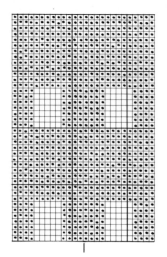

*Mid-front and mid-
half of the back,
mid-sleeve*

● = *garter stitch*
□ = *stockinette stitch*

NUMBER OF STITCHES AND ROWS BETWEEN THE SQUARES
15 stitches/30 rows (17 stitches/34
rows) 19 stitches/38 rows

When the 5th square has been
reached, cast off the 3 left-hand
edge stitches.

When the 7th square has been
reached, start casting off for the
neckline: 2 stitches inside the edge
stitch are knitted together every
second row 8 (10) 12 times. The edge
stitch is knitted as before.

Cast off 10 (12) 14 stitches at the
same side as the neckline shaping.
The remaining stitches are placed on
a spare needle or safety pin.

The second front piece is knitted
in the same way, but reversed.

BACK
Cast on 119 (131) 143 stitches.

Knit 26 rows in garter stitch. Slip
3 stitches at each side and in the
center every other row with the
wrong side facing, keeping the yarn
forward. This means knitting 58 (64)
70 stitches before slipping the 3
center stitches.

Knit the pattern according to the
diagram.

When the 5th square has been
reached, cast off the 3 edge stitches
at each end.

When the back piece measures 7
squares and 16 (20) 24 rows, cast off
the 37 (45) 53 center stitches.

Knit the front and back shoulder
stitches together, casting off at the
same time (see p. 115).

SLEEVES

Cast on 61 (67) 73 stitches.

Knit 26 rows in garter stitch and slip 3 stitches at each end, with the wrong side facing and yarn forward.

Knit the pattern according to the diagram and, if possible, place the squares according to the same system as for front and back, making sure that the center of the sleeve is between two squares.

Increase by 1 stitch at each end inside the 3 edge stitches every 8th row.

Cast off when the sleeve measures 4 squares and 22 rows.

FINISHING

Join the sleeve to the front and back pieces, with the center of the sleeve matching the shoulder seam.

Join the sleeve seams and side seams.

If desired, 5 to 6 loops may be crocheted on the inside of the left front and buttons sewn to the corresponding place on the inside of the right front to form a hidden buttoning device.

Garland, Streak and Little Knot

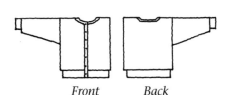

Front　　*Back*

Front　　*Back*

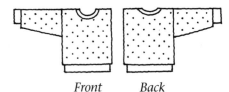

Front　　*Back*

Garland is the inevitable result of my fascination with patterns, which has made it into a rather complicated mixture of knitting techniques. Knitting *Garland* is, however, by no means unfeasible. Several colors are used in the same row, and some of them only within a restricted area. This means that there will often be a great distance between stitches of the same color, so that the yarn will have to be woven in, or preferably sewn onto the wrong side after the knitting has been done. I have solved the problem of this rather unattractive and tangled inside of the cardigan by lining it with fabric. This also makes it more comfortable to wear.

The back features the same patterns as the sleeves, broken in the middle by a narrow border just like the sides. The purl stitches provide an interesting texture among the multicolored patterns.

Streak is described on p. 116

Streak is described on p. 116

The *Little Knot* sweater is easy to knit and lends itself to other color combinations. The little knot that has given the sweater its name is a Norwegian-style louse pattern, which is knitted over two rows and done in a purl stitch in one of these rows.

*Diagram for
front and back*

□ = *white*
× = *greenish turquoise*
■ = *red knit stitch*
/ = *green*
◢ = *yellowish green*
| = *turquoise*
∨ = *yellow*
– = *reddish yellow*
⌐ = *red purl stitch*
● = *white purl stitch*

| *Center-back stitch* *Side* |

Garland

MEASUREMENTS (CHEST SIZE)

84cm/33 in.

YARN

Fingering-weight yarn
Natural white: 2½ 100g balls [9 oz.];
Greenish turquoise: ½ 100g ball
[1¾ oz.]; Red: ¼ 100g ball [1 oz.];
Green: a small quantity; Yellowish
green: a small quantity; Turquoise: a
small quantity; Yellow: a small
quantity; Reddish yellow: a small
quantity

NEEDLES

1 circular needle in sizes 2½mm (U.S.
1-2, U.K. 12-13) and 3mm (U.S. 2-3,
U.K. 11), 1 set of double-pointed
needles in sizes 2½mm (U.S. 1-2,
U.K. 12-13) and 3mm (U.S. 2-3, U.K.
11) and 1 pair of needles size 3mm
(U.S. 2-3, U.K. 11)

GAUGE

30 stitches to 10cm/4 in. It is
recommended to knit a gauge
sample; should your gauge differ
from the one indicated, change to
smaller or larger needles.

FRONT AND BACK

Using the smaller circular needle and
white yarn, cast on 208 stitches. The
cardigan sweater is knitted in the
round and is cut at the mid-front; 6
of the 208 stitches make up the seam
allowance.

Knit 16 rows in stockinette stitch,
i.e., knit stitches, followed by 1 purl row.

Knit the lower edge pattern
according to the diagram on p. 108.

Change to white yarn again and
knit 4 rows in stockinette stitch,
increasing the number of stitches by
47 over the first of these rows.

Change to the larger circular
needle and knit the rest of the
sweater according to the diagram.

SLEEVES

Using the smaller double-pointed
needles and white yarn, cast on 49
stitches. Knit 16 rows in stockinette
stitch, followed by 1 purl row.

Knit the cuff pattern according to
the diagram on p. 108.

The rest of the sleeve is knitted
according to the sleeve diagram on
p. 108. Alternatively, the sleeves may
be knitted from top to bottom, i.e.
starting from stitches picked up
around the armhole and finishing by
knitting the cuff according to the
instructions above.

FRONT BAND

Stitches for the front and neck band
are picked up after the cutting and
hemming at the mid-front.

Using the smaller circular needle,
pick up about 290 stitches (94 at each
front edge and 102 at the neckline).

Knit 1 row from the wrong side,
using knit stitches and greenish-
turquoise yarn, followed by 1 row in
knit stitches and red yarn from the
right side. Knit 3 rows in stockinette
stitch and white yarn. In every row,
increase by 1 stitch at each side of the
stitch between the front band and the
neck band. Make 6 buttonholes in
the right front band over 2 rows; then
knit 4 rows in stockinette stitch.

Purl 1 row from the right side to
make a hemline.

The inside of the front band is
then knitted in the same number of
rows as the outside, but striped in 2
rows of red and 2 rows of green.
Buttonholes are made in the same
places as on the outside band.
Decreases are made, corresponding to
the increases at the "corners."

FINISHING

Using the purl hemline, fold the
lower edge, cuff edges and the front
and neck bands to the wrong side
and slip stitch in place.

Garland

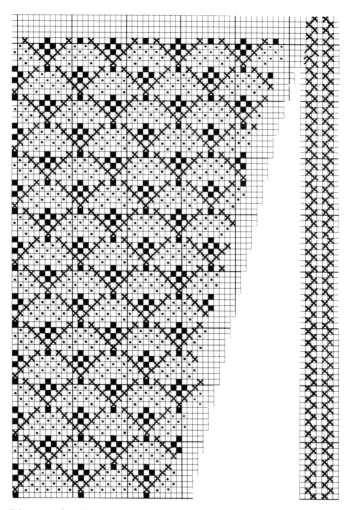

Diagram for sleeve
center stitch

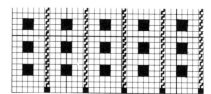

Diagram for cuff

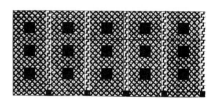

Diagram for lower edge

Little Knot

MEASUREMENTS (CHEST SIZE)

Children's sizes: Small: 72cm/28½ in. (Medium: 81cm/32 in.)
Large: 90cm/35½ in.

NUMBER OF PATTERN REPEATS (MULTIPLES OF 12)

16 (18) 20. Add or subtract 2 repeats when adapting the size.

YARN

Fingering-weight yarn
Green: 2 (2½) 3 100g balls [7 oz. (9 oz.) 10½ oz.]; White: ¼ (¼) ¼ 100g ball [1 oz. (1 oz.) 1 oz.]

NEEDLES

1 circular needle in sizes 2½mm (U.S. 1-2, U.K. 12-13) and 3mm (U.S. 2-3, U.K. 11), 1 set of double-pointed needles in sizes 2½mm (U.S. 1-2, U.K. 12-13) and 3mm (U.S. 2-3, U.K. 11) and 1 pair of needles in size 3mm (U.S. 2-3, U.K. 11)

GAUGE

Ribbing: 28 stitches to 10cm/4 in.; stockinette: 25 stitches to 10cm/4 in. It is recommended to knit a gauge sample; should your gauge differ from the one indicated, change to smaller or larger needles.

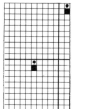

1 pattern repeat

☐ = green
■ = white knit stitch
● = white purl stitch

FRONT AND BACK

Using the smaller circular needle and green yarn, cast on 176 (196) 216 stitches.

Knit the ribbing (1 knit, 1 purl) for 15 (17) 19 rows.

Change to the larger circular needle and increase the number of stitches by 16 (20) 24 over the first row. Knit the pattern according to the diagram.

When work measures 3½ (4) 4 vertical pattern repeats, divide for front and back, each piece to be knitted separately.

Starting with the front, knit 1½ (1½) 2 pattern repeats plus another 5 to 6 rows.

Place the 11 (13) 15 center stitches on a spare needle or piece of yarn for the front neckline.

Knit each side separately and cast off: 4-3-2-1-1 (4-3-2-1-1-1) 5-3-2-1-1-1 stitches at the neckline.

Knit another 6 rows without shaping.

Do not cast off but put the remaining stitches on a spare needle or piece of yarn.

For the back, knit 2 (2) 2½ pattern repeats.

Place the 25 (27) 29 center stitches on a spare needle or piece of yarn. Knit each side separately and cast off: 2-1-1 (2-1-1-1) 2-1-1-1-1 stitches.

Do not cast off the shoulder stitches but knit them together from the wrong side with those of the front, casting off at the same time (see p. 115).

SLEEVES

Using the larger double-pointed needles, pick up about 80 (84) 100 stitches around the armhole. Knit the pattern according to the diagram.

Decrease 1 stitch every 4th row on each side of the center stitch (under the arm).

Knit 4 (4½) 5 pattern repeats plus another 8 rows.

Before changing to ribbing, decrease the number of stitches to 46 (50) 54.

Change to the smaller double-pointed needles and knit the ribbing (1 knit, 1 purl) for 10 (12) 14 rows. Cast off.

NECKBAND

Using the smaller double-pointed needles, pick up about 90 (100) 110 stitches and knit ribbing for 8 (9) 10 rows. Cast off.

Rainbow and Dawn

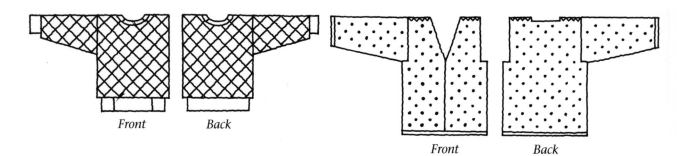

Front   *Back*

Front   *Back*

The technique used in the *Rainbow* sweater is referred to as diagonal patchwork (entrelac) knitting (see p. 31 and p. 134). *Rainbow* has, as it were, two fronts, to be used according to taste and wish. Consequently, the neckline shaping is identical on both sides.

The texture of the knitting should be firm, which sets off the technique more clearly and attractively. In the instructions I have not indicated the exact distribution of the colors, since I prefer to leave it to your imagination.

Knitting with as many shades of color as in this sweater results in a great number of loose ends to be fastened, but it should not be too much of a burden, especially if done continuously. It is, in fact, possible to fasten the yarn automatically at one end by picking up stitches with double (folded) yarn.

The bottom (i.e., around the hips), neckline and wrist edges are picked up and knitted at the end. In order to make them match the colors of the sweater, you may want to knit them in several overlapping parts (see the photo on the facing page).

Dawn is quite like its source of inspiration, the Forsa sweater on p. 37. However, for this jacket I have changed the colors as well as the design. What does remain from the original is the two-color pattern and the attractive textured edge pattern consisting of four purl rows with two strands of yarn and floating stitches on the right side.

Rainbow

MEASUREMENTS (CHEST SIZE)

Medium: 106cm/42 in.
The squares are knitted over 8 stitches. A smaller size is achieved by knitting 7-stitch squares, a larger by knitting 9-stitch squares.

YARN

Sport-weight yarn in the colors of the rainbow.

NEEDLES

1 circular needle in size 2½mm (U.S. 1-2, U.K. 12-13) and 1 set of double-pointed needles in size 2½mm (U.S. 1-2, U.K. 12-13)

GAUGE

1 8-stitch square to about 2½cm/1 in. horizontally. Garter stitch: 24 stitches to 10cm/4 in. It is recommended to knit a gauge sample; should your gauge differ from the one indicated, change to smaller or larger needles.

FRONT AND BACK

Knit all the half squares at the lower edge of the sweater for the circumference of the whole sweater.

Knit all the ◇ squares. The last square is joined together with the last square farthest to the right. Begin knitting in the round.

Continue knitting squares according to the diagram.

When the thick line indicated on the diagram has been reached, divide and start knitting back and forth.

After completion, the two parts should be knitted together at the shoulders.

SLEEVES

Then pick up stitches and knit the sleeve from top to bottom, starting with the square in the middle, i.e., at the shoulder line and knit the round of half squares as shown in the diagram.

Knit 7 repeats of 8-stitch squares. The narrowing of the sleeve is achieved by picking up 1 stitch fewer per square and knitting 1 of these stitches together with 2 from the preceding round of squares. Continue knitting 6 rounds of 7-stitch squares, 5 rounds of 6-stitch squares and 2½ rounds of 5-stitch squares.

FINISHING

Pick up stitches for the garter-stitch edges (lower, neck and wrist), 24 stitches to 10cm/4 in.

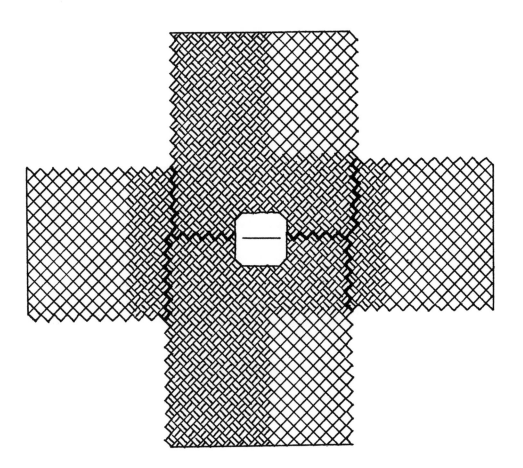

$\triangle$ = Cast on 2 stitches. Starting with the second half-square, knit these stitches before Row 1.
Row 1: Purl 2. Row 2: Increase 1, knit 2. Row 3: Purl 3. Row 4: Increase 1, knit 3. Row 5: Purl 4. Row 6: Increase 1, knit 4. Row 7: Purl 5, etc., until achieving the desired number of stitches, in this case, 8.

$\diamondsuit$ = Pick up 8 stitches along the left side of the last half square.
Row 1: Purl 8. Row 2: Knit 7, knit 1 stitch together with 1 stitch of the half-square to the left (make sure the stitch is not twisted). Row 3: Slip 1, purl 7. Repeat rows 2 and 3 until there are no more stitches in the half square.

$\diamondsuit$ = Knit as for the square with the reversed diagonal line, but the knitting together should be done with 1 purl stitch and the wrong side facing. Starting with the second square, pick up the stitches with the wrong side facing, i.e., the needle is put through the knitting from the right side and the yarn is pulled from the wrong side to the right side.

$\bigtriangledown$ = At the side of the square where there is no knitting together, cast off 1 stitch at the beginning of the row, i.e., every second row.

$\triangleleft$ = nearest stitch in the square to the left.
Row 1: Purl 1. Row 2: Increase 1, 1 knitting together. Row 3: Purl 2. Row 4: Increase 1, knit 1, 1 knitting together. Row 5: Purl 3. Row 6: Increase 1, knit 2, 1 knitting together, etc., until there are no more stitches in the whole square. The number of stitches in the new half square should now be 8.

$\triangleright$ = Pick up 8 stitches as before. There is no knitting together. At the edge of the square that is to be vertical, cast off 1 stitch at the beginning of every other row.

Dawn

MEASUREMENTS (CHEST SIZE)
Small: 100cm/39½ in.
(Medium: 110cm/43½ in.)
Large: 120cm/47 in.

YARN
Fingering-weight yarn
Light grey or beige: 5 (6) 7 100g balls
[18 oz. (21 oz.) 25 oz.]; for the other
18 shades, which should be selected
from the colors of the rainbow: ¼ (¼)
¼ 100g ball [1 oz. (1 oz.) 1 oz.]. See
the photo on p. 111 for the
distribution of colors.

NEEDLES
1 pair in size 3mm (U.S. 2-3, U.K. 11)

GAUGE
35 stitches to 10cm/4 in. It is
recommended to knit a gauge sample;
should your gauge differ from the one
indicated, change to smaller or larger
needles.

LEFT FRONT
Using the main color, cast on 85 (97)
109 stitches.
    *Purl 1 row, followed by a purl row
on the right side, using two strands of
yarn; every other stitch is purled with
one strand and every other stitch
with the other strand. The yarn is
kept forward, i.e., in front of the
knitting, and when a stitch is purled,
the yarn is kept outside the stitch
that has already been purled.*
    Repeat from * to * 3 times.
    Knit 7 rows in stockinette stitch
before beginning with the pattern
according to the diagram. Change
colors for every row of patterns.
    When 5½ pattern repeats have
been completed, cast off for the
neckline at the right side and for the
armhole at the left side.

The neckline, 1 stitch is cast off
every 5th row. For the armhole, 18
(23) 28 stitches are cast off.
    The left side is knitted straight,
without shaping.
    Continue casting off for the
neckline until 52 (56) 60 stitches
remain on the needle. The work
should then measure 9 vertical
pattern repeats. Using the
main color, knit 2 rows before the
shoulder border.
    Knit the shoulder border according
to the diagram.
    Do not cast off. Put the stitches on
a spare needle or piece of yarn.

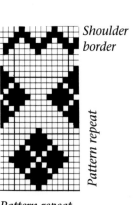

Pattern repeat
Size Small

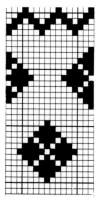

Shoulder border

Pattern repeat
Size Medium

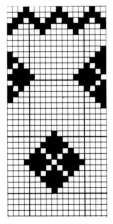

Pattern repeat
Size Large

RIGHT FRONT

Knit as for left front, with the armhole and neckline on the reversed sides.

BACK

Using the main color, cast on 169 (193) 217 stitches.

Knit the lower edge pattern according to the diagram, then cast off for the armhole as for the front.

When 9 vertical pattern repeats have been completed, cast off the 29 (35) 41 center stitches.

Using the main color, knit 2 rows on each side of the cast-off stitches, followed by the shoulder border, the patterns matching the border on the front.

Do not cast off. Put the stitches on a spare needle or piece of yarn.

SLEEVES

Using the main color, cast on 99 (113) 127 stitches.

Knit the edge as on the other parts. Follow the diagram, starting with color 3 (see the photo on p. 111).

Increase by 1 stitch at each end about every 9th row.

Add pattern shapes when the number of stitches allows it.

When the sleeve measured 6 vertical pattern repeats, knit 16 (20) 24 rows without shaping. Cast off.

FINISHING

Knit the shoulder stitches together, casting off at the same time.

Put the stitches back onto the needles. Place the front pieces on the back piece, the right sides facing. Using a third needle, knit 1 stitch from the front together with 1 stitch from the back. Repeat. Cast off 1 stitch. Repeat until there are no stitches left.

Knit a stockinette-stitch band for the front edges and neckline of the jacket:

Using the main color, cast on 10 stitches. Keep knitting until the band measures the same length as the front edges and neckline. Sew the band onto the jacket, fold to the wrong side and slip stitch in place.

Join the sleeves to the front and back.

Crochet 4 to 5 loops on the left front in the seam joining the band to the edge. Sew the same number of buttons onto the right front band; this will make the buttoning invisible.

Streak

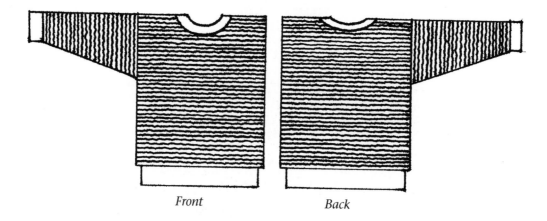

Front   *Back*

Streak represents extreme simplicity in pattern design. It is, in fact, an ideal sweater for beginners. All stitches are done knitwise. The colors can easily be changed. Bear in mind, however, that one color should be darker than the other.

Streak is derived from the patterned garter-stitch lower edge of the Delsbo and Bjuråker sweaters (see pp. 51-55). Although my adaptation is extremely simple, the pattern technique is certainly worth developing.

Streak

MEASUREMENTS
(CHEST SIZE)
Children: 60cm/23½ in. (70cm/27½ in.)
80/31½ in. (90cm/35½ in.)
Small: 100cm/39½ in.
(Medium: 110cm/43½ in.)
Large: 120cm/47 in.
(Extra large: 130cm/51 in.)

YARN
Worsted-weight yarn
Brown: 3 (3) 4 (4) 5 (6) 7 (8) 100g
balls [10½ oz. (10½ oz.) 14 oz. (14 oz.)
17½ oz. (21 oz.) 24½ oz. (28 oz.];
Black: 2 (2) 3 (3) 4 (5) 6 (6) 100g balls
[7 oz. (7 oz.) 10½ oz. (10½ oz.) 14 oz.
(17½ oz.) 21 oz. (21 oz.)]

NEEDLES
1 pair in sizes 3½mm (U.S. 4, U.K. 9-
10) and 4mm (U.S. 5-6, U.K. 8) and 1
set of double-pointed needles in size
3½mm (U.S. 4, U.K. 9-10)

GAUGE
20 stitches to 10cm/4 in. It is
recommended to knit a gauge
sample; should your gauge differ
from the one indicated, change to
smaller or larger needles.

FRONT
Using the smaller needles and brown
yarn, cast on 64 (74) 84 (94) 104
(114) 124 (134) stitches.

Knit 19 (19) 21 (23) 25 (27) 29 (31)
rows in garter stitch.

Change to the larger needles and
knit 2 rows in garter stitch using
brown yarn, followed by 2 rows using
black yarn. Repeat these 4 rows.

When work measures 35cm/14 in.
(40cm/15½ in.) 46cm/18 in.
(50cm/19½ in.) 54cm/21½ in.
(57cm/22½ in.) 60cm/23½ in.
(63cm/25 in.) or desired length,
begin shaping the neckline:

Place the 8 (8) 10 (10) 12 (12) 14
(14) center stitches on a spare needle
or safety pin.

Cast off on each side of the center
stitches, every other row: 4-3-2-1-1
(4-3-2-1-1-1) 4-3-2-1-1-1 (4-3-2-1-1-1-1)
4-3-2-1-1-1 (4-3-2-1-1-1-1) 5-3-2-
1-1-1-1-1 (5-3-2-1-1-1-1-1)

Knit another 4 (4) 6 (6) 8 (8) 10
(10) rows on each side. Cast off.

BACK
Knit as for front, but the work
should measure 37cm/14½ in.
(43cm/17 in.) 49cm/19 in. (53cm/21 in.)
57cm/22½ in. (61cm/24 in.)
65cm/25½ in. (68cm/27 in.) up to
the neckline. Make sure that the
number of stripes is the same for
front and back when casting off the
shoulder stitches.

For the neckline: Put the 22 (22) 24
(24) 26 (26) 28 (28) center stitches on
a spare needle or safety pin. Cast off
at each side: 2-1-1 (2-1-1-1) 2-1-1-1
(3-2-1-1) 3-2-1-1 (3-2-1-1) 4-3-2-1
(4-3-2-1).

Cast off the remaining stitches.

SLEEVE
Using the smaller needles and brown
yarn, cast on 36 (40) 40 (44) 50 (56)
60 (60) stitches, knit 15 (15) 15 (15)
17 (17) 17 (19) rows in garter stitch.
Change to brown yarn and increase
by 6 (6) 6 (6) 6 (8) 8 (10) stitches over
the first of these rows. Knit 2 rows in
garter stitch using black yarn.
Increase 1 stitch at each side every
9th row until there are 62 (68) 76 (84)
92 (108) 116 (122) stitches on the
needle. Cast off when the sleeve
measures 25cm/10 in. (26cm/10½ in.)
32cm/12½ in. (38cm/15 in.) 43cm/17 in.
(49cm/19 in.) 55cm/21½ in.
(60cm/23½ in.). Cast off.

NECKLINE
Using double-pointed needles and
brown yarn, pick up about 70 (70) 80
(80) 100 (100) 118 (118) stitches.
Knitting in the round, begin by
purling 1 row then knitting 1 row,
etc., for 9 (9) 11 (11) 13 (13) 15 (15)
rows. Cast off. Join all seams.

Streak also lends itself to practicing the use of paper patterns for knitting, done according to individual measurements. Make the pattern like this:

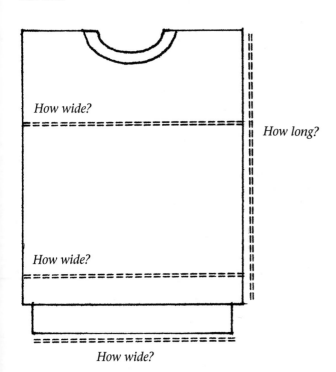

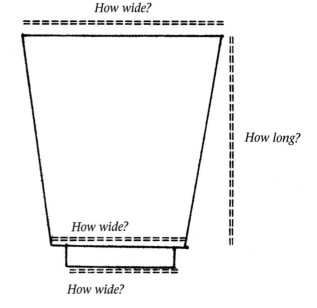

Cut out the neckline a bit too small and fit it in front of a mirror.

Put the sweater on the pattern pieces to determine the increase of the arm width.

Dove

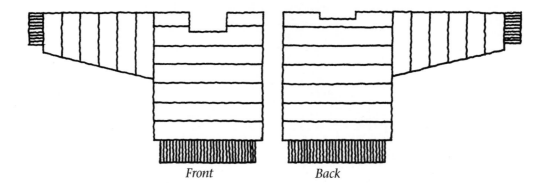

Front   Back

The sweater features the same pattern as the Järvsö sweater on p. 41, which is one of the most beautiful sweaters I have ever seen and has become my absolute favorite.

Since I find the checkerboard squares interesting in combination with other patterns but preferred to do the lower edges in ribbing, I have used the squares as shoulder borders.

Dove

MEASUREMENTS
(CHEST SIZE)
Small: 90cm/35½ in.
(Medium: 110cm/43½ in.)
Large: 130cm/51 in.

YARN
Fingering-weight yarn
Dark grey: 2 (2½) 3 100g balls [7 oz.
(9 oz.) 10½ oz.]; Black: 2 (2½) 3
100g balls [7 oz. (9 oz.) 10½ oz.];
Light grey: 1 (1) 1 100g ball [3½ oz.
(3½ oz.) 3½ oz.]

NEEDLES
1 circular needle in sizes 2mm (U.S. 0,
U.K. 14) and 3mm (U.S. 2-3, U.K. 11),
1 set of double-pointed needles in
sizes 2mm (U.S. 0, U.K. 14) and 3mm
(U.S. 2-3, U.K. 11) and 1 pair of
needles in size 3mm (U.S. 2-3, U.K. 11)

GAUGE
Ribbing: 32 stitches to 10cm/4 in.;
two-color stockinette stitch: 28
stitches to 10cm/4 in. It is recommended
to knit a gauge sample; should your
gauge differ from the one indicated,
change to smaller or larger needles.

FRONT AND BACK
Using the smaller circular needles and
light grey yarn, cast on 260 (312) 364
stitches.

1 repeat

□ = *dark grey*
■ = *black*
● = *light grey*

Checkerboard pattern for the back

*Simultaneous knitting together and
casting off of the shoulder stitches*

Checkerboard pattern for the front

Knit 32 (37) 42 rows in ribbing:
purl 1, knit 1.

Change to the larger circular
needle and knit the pattern
according to the diagram. Repeat 10
(12) 14 times.

When work measures 2 vertical
pattern repeats plus 16 rows (3
pattern repeats plus 8 rows) 4 pattern
repeats, divide for front and back.
Knit each piece separately, starting
with the front.

When work measures 4 repeats
plus 16 rows (5 repeats plus 16 rows)
6 repeats plus 12 rows, cast off the 40
(48) 56 center stitches for the front
neckline. Knit each shoulder piece
straight, i.e., without shaping, and
when the repeat is completed,
proceed to knit the checkerboard-
square pattern according to the
diagram.

Do not cast off. Put the shoulder
stitches on a spare needle or a piece
of yarn.

Knit the back, When it measures 5 (6) 7 repeats plus 8 rows in the squares pattern, cast off the 40 (48) 56 center stitches for the back neckline. Knit each shoulder piece straight, i.e., without shaping, and knit the pattern according to the diagram.

Knit the shoulder stitches together, casting off at the same time (see p. 115).

SLEEVES
Using the larger double-pointed needles and dark grey yarn, pick up about 120 (136) 152 stitches around the armhole.

Knit the pattern according to the diagram. Decrease 1 stitch every 5th row on each side of the center stitch (under the arm).

When the sleeve measures 5 (6) 7 pattern repeats, decrease the number of stitches over the last row so that 60 (70) 84 stitches remain on the needles.

Changing to the smaller double-pointed needles and light grey yarn, knit the ribbing (knit 1, purl 1) for 22 (26) 30 rows. Cast off.

NECKBAND
Pick up the same number of stitches as were cast off at the front neckline. Purl 1 row from the right side for the hemline and then knit 10 rows in stockinette stitch, increasing 1 stitch at each end on the knit rows. Cast off, and knit the same band for the back.

Pick up 36 (36) 40 stitches along the 2 other sides of the neckline and knit the band as before.

Fold the bands to the wrong side of the hemline and slip stitch in place.

123

Shirt and Moss

Shirt is knitted in garter stitch and cotton yarn with a pattern in stockinette stitch and woolen yarn. The mixture of wool and cotton, as well as the design of the pattern, is related to the Bjuråker sweater on p. 51. Its checked garter-stitch pattern at the lower edge, where the white component is in cotton, led to these striped rectangular shapes. It is, of course, perfectly possible to knit *Shirt* exclusively in wool or cotton.

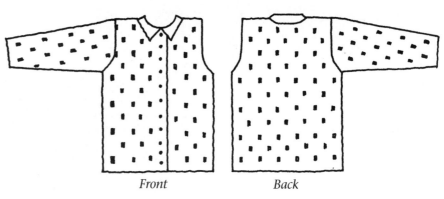

Front   *Back*

The *Moss* sweater represents extreme simplicity. The whole sweater is knitted in moss stitch, including the lower and sleeve edges, which have a firmer texture. The sleeve features only one decorative pattern: the side and sleeve seams are marked by 8 garter stitches, breaking the moss pattern. It goes without saying that *Moss* may be knitted in any color.

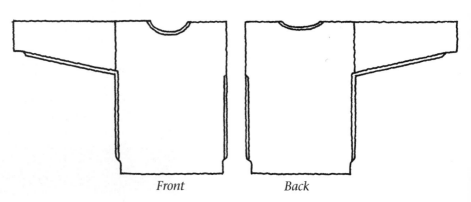

Front   *Back*

Shirt

MEASUREMENTS
(CHEST SIZE)
Small: 100cm/39½ in.
(Medium: 110cm/43½ in.)
Large: 120cm/47 in.

YARN
Fingering-weight unbleached
cotton yarn 8/4
7 (8) 9 100g balls [24½ oz. (28 oz.)
31½ oz.]
Fingering-weight yarn
Small quantities of each color: Yellow,
Red, Light blue, Dark blue, Green

NEEDLES
1 pair in size 2½mm (U.S. 1-2, U.K.
12-13)

GAUGE
30 stitches to 10cm/4 in.

LEFT FRONT
Cast on 77 (91) 105 stitches. Knit 29
(37) 41 rows in garter stitch.

Knit the pattern according to the
diagram, starting after the first 11 (13)
15 stitches on the right-hand side.

When the front measures 3 vertical
pattern repeats plus 1 rectangular
pattern shape, cast off for the
armhole: 4-3-2-2-1-1-1-1 (4-3-3-2-1-
1-1-1) 5-4-3-2-1-1-1-1-1 stitches.

When the front measures 5 pattern
repeats, cast off for the neckline:

PATTERN DIAGRAM

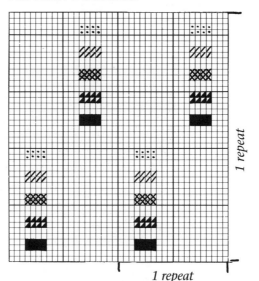

□ = *garter stitch*
● = *yellow stocking stitch*
/ = *red stocking stitch*
× = *light blue stocking stitch*
◢ = *dark blue stocking stitch*
■ = *green stocking stitch*

NUMBER OF STITCHES AND ROWS BETWEEN THE PATTERN SHAPES
20 stitches/38 rows (24 stitches/46 rows) 28 stitches/54 rows
Note that the diagram only sets out the relative distribution of the
patterns. Note also that the number of rows refers to pattern shapes
in the same vertical line.

14-4-3-2-1-1-1-1 (17-4-3-2-2-1-1-1-1-1)
22-4-3-3-2-2-1-1-1-1-1 stitches.

Cast off for a sloping shoulder line
by dividing the number of stitches
into three and casting off a third at
the armhole edge every second row.

RIGHT FRONT
Knit as for left front, but reversed.

Start making buttonholes after the
first 7 stitches on the right-hand side
at the same time as the pattern
begins. Cast off 2 to 3 stitches,
depending on the desired size of the

button, and cast on the same number of stitches in the following row.

Make the buttonholes at intervals of 38 (46) 54 rows, i.e., 7 buttonholes.

BACK
Cast on 146 (170) 194 stitches. Knit 29 (37) 41 rows in garter stitch.

Knit the pattern according to the diagram, starting after the first 11 (13) 15 stitches.

When the back measures 3 vertical pattern repeats plus 1 rectangular pattern shape, cast off at both sides for the armhole as indicated for the front pieces.

When the back measures 5 pattern repeats plus 10 (14) 18 rows, cast off for the neckline. Place the 26 (34) 46 center stitches onto a spare needle or safety pin.

Knit each shoulder piece separately and continue casting off for the neckline by 4-3-2-1 stitches.

Cast off the shoulder stitches as for the front pieces.

SLEEVES
Cast on 64 (76) 88 stitches. Knit 16 (24) 28 rows in garter stitch before changing to the pattern according to the diagram. Increase the width of the sleeve by 1 stitch at each end every 5th row. When the sleeve measures 3 vertical pattern repeats plus 18 (22) 26 rows, the number of stitches should amount to about 116 (136) 156. Start casting off for the armhole shaping. The shaping should be made in the same way on each side:
22x1, 2x2, 2x3, 2x4, 5 stitches
(23x1, 2x2, 2x3, 2x4, 2x5 stitches)
25x1, 2x2, 2x3, 2x4, 3x5 stitches

Cast off the remaining stitches.

FINISHING
Join the side seams and shoulder seams.

Sew in the sleeve, making adjustments if necessary to make a good fit.

Sew on the buttons.

COLLAR
From the wrong side, pick up about 100 (115) 135 stitches, beginning and ending 7 (9) 11 stitches from the front edges.

Knit 44 (50) 56 rows in garter stitch. Cast off.

Moss

MEASUREMENTS (CHEST SIZE)
Small: 100cm/39½ in.
(Medium: 112cm/44 in.)
Large: 125cm/49 in.

YARN
Worsted-weight yarn
9 (10) 11 100g balls [31½ oz. (35½ oz.) 39 oz.]

NEEDLES
1 pair in sizes 3mm (U.S. 2-3, U.K. 11) and 3½mm (U.S. 4, U.K. 9-10) and 1 set of double-pointed needles in size 3mm (U.S. 2-3, U.K. 11)

GAUGE
20 stitches to 10cm/4 in.; edges: 22 stitches to 10cm/4 in. It is recommended to knit a gauge sample; should your gauge differ from the one indicated, change to smaller or larger needles.

FRONT
Using the smaller needles, cast on 110 (120) 130) stitches.

Knit 22 (24) 26 rows in moss stitch, i.e., knit 1, purl 1, repeated to the end of the row. In the following row, knit stitches are purled and purl stitches are knitted.

Change to the larger needles. Knit 8 stitches at each end in garter stitch and the rest in moss stitch.

When work measures 41cm/16 in. (43cm/17 in.) 45cm/17½ in., cast off the 8 garter stitches at each end.

Place the 12 (14) 16 center stitches on a spare needle or safety pin.

Knit the shoulder pieces separately, continuing the casting off for the neckline: 4-3-2-1.

Knit 10 (12) 14 rows without shaping.

Do not cast off. Put the shoulder stitches on a spare needle or safety pin.

BACK
Using the smaller needles, cast on 102 (112) 122 stitches. Knit 22 (24) 26 rows in moss stitch.

Change to the larger needles and continue knitting moss stitch over all the stitches.

When work measures 63cm/25 in. (67cm/26½ in.) 71cm/28 in., place the 20 (22) 24 center stitches onto a spare needle or safety pin.

Knit each shoulder piece separately, continuing the casting off for the neckline by 3-2-1 stitches.

Knit the shoulder stitches for back and front together, casting off at the same time (see p. 115).

SLEEVES
Using the smaller needles, cast on 46 (50) 54 stitches and knit 16 (18) 20 rows in moss stitch.

Change to thicker needles and increase 10 (12) 14 stitches over the knit row.

Knit 8 stitches at one side of the sleeve in garter stitch as for the front.

Increase 1 stitch at the side without the garter-stitch band and 1 stitch between the garter stitch and the moss stitch at the other end; repeat the increase every 7th row.

When the sleeve measures 44cm/17½ in. (48cm/18 in.) 52cm/20½ in. long and is about 44cm/17½ in. (50cm/19½ in.) 56cm/22 in. wide, cast off.

FINISHING
Join the side seams and sleeve seams.

Sew in the sleeves, making sure that the garter-stitch bands match.

NECKBAND
Using double-pointed needles, pick up about 80 (88) 95 stitches. Purl 2 rows from the right side. Cast off.

Forest

Forest

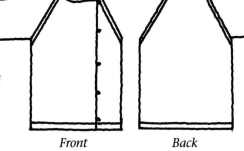

Front   *Back*

Märta Stina Abrahamsdotter's coverlet on p. 63 is the source of inspiration for the *Forest* jacket. The jacket is knitted in rug yarn, the current-day yarn that corresponds most closely to the yarn Märta Stina used in knitting her coverlets.

The jacket is as heavy as an old coat. In order to make it warm, windproof and less prickly, it should be lined.

Lining the jacket will also do away with the worry about floating stitches on the wrong side. Nevertheless, it's a good idea to weave the yarn not in use around the working yarn from time to time.

MEASUREMENTS (CHEST SIZE)
116cm/45½ in.

YARN
Worsted-weight rug yarn
Purple: 3 100g balls [10½ oz.]; Dark turquoise: 2½ 100g balls [9 oz.]; Wine color: 3 100g balls [10½ oz.]; Green: 1 100g ball [3½ oz.]; Turquoise: 4 100g balls [14 oz.]; Brick red: ½ 100g ball [1¾ oz.]

NEEDLES
1 pair in size 3½mm (U.S. 4, U.K. 9-10)

GAUGE
22 stitches to 10cm/4 in. It is recommended to knit a gauge sample; should your gauge differ from the one indicated, change to smaller or larger needles.

FRONT, BACK AND SLEEVES
Using green yarn, cast on stitches according to the diagrams.

For the front, cast on the number of stitches from the side seam to the folding line.

Knit the jacket according to the diagrams on pp. 131-133, but begin by knitting 8 rows in stockinette stitch and 1 purl row from the right side.

When the green edge is completed, cast on 10 stitches at the edges of both front pieces to be folded in after the work has been completed.

The vertical green stitches are knitted with separate balls of yarn. Twist the yarn ends when changing colors.

FINISHING
Join the side seams and sleeve seams and the green stitches at the shoulder. Sew in the sleeves.

Fold the front edges according to the diagram and slip stitch in place.

Fold the lower edges to the wrong side at the purled hemline and slip stitch in place.

Using green yarn, pick up about 110 stitches around the neckline from one folded edge to the other. Purl 1 row from the right side, followed by 8 rows in stockinette stitch. Cast off. Fold to the wrong side and slip stitch in place. Line the garment. On the right front piece, crochet 5 loops to be used as buttonholes. Sew on buttons to the left front piece.

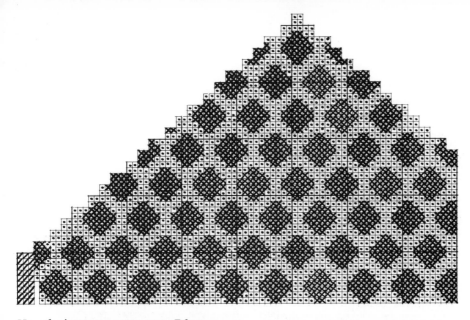

Here the increases occur every 7th row.

Diagram for sleeve
■ = *purple*
● = *turquoise (front and back)*
✕ = *wine*
● = *dark turquoise (sleeve)*
/ = *green*
□ = *brick red*

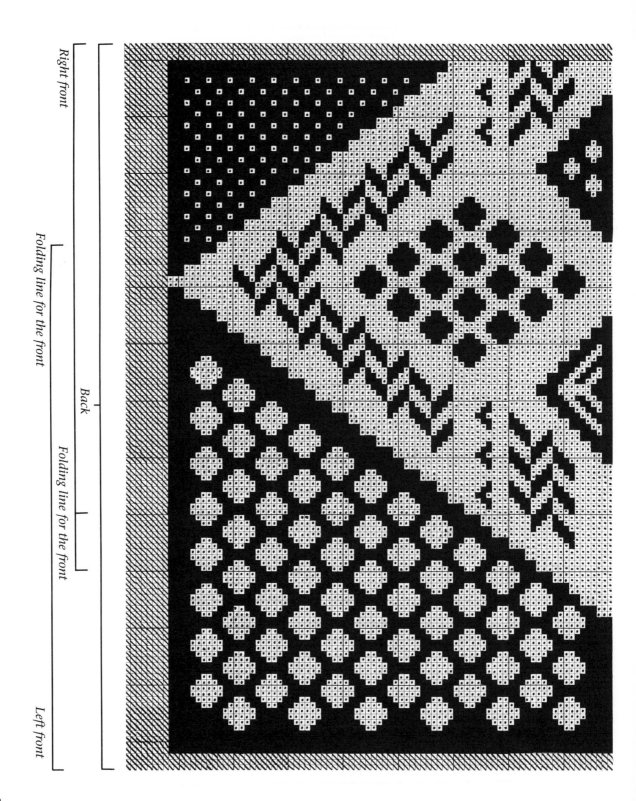

Right front

Folding line for the front

Back

Folding line for the front

Left front

Sailor and Mate

The pattern used for *Sailor* is a combination of two-color stockinette stitch and moss stitch. The stripe is a detail adapted from the Delsbo and Bjuråker sweaters.

Sailor has no seams at all; at the shoulder the stitches have been knitted together and cast off at the same time; the sleeve has been picked up and knitted in the round from top to bottom.

The colors of *Sailor* can be changed easily. For example, keep the white and combine it with almost any other color. If both colors are changed, one should be lighter or brighter than the other.

The photo shows *Sailor* in a child's size; there are also instructions for adult sizes.

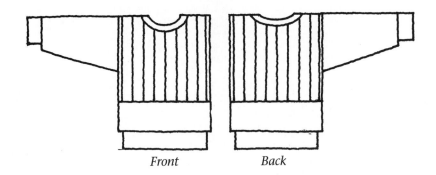

Front   *Back*

Mate is done in diagonal patchwork (entrelac) knitting (see p. 31 and p. 110). The whole garment is knitted in stockinette stitch, which sets off the plaited texture.

Mate is a soft and warm sweater, suitable for outdoor wear on a chilly summer evening, as a weapon against the cold of winter, or as an indoor energy saver.

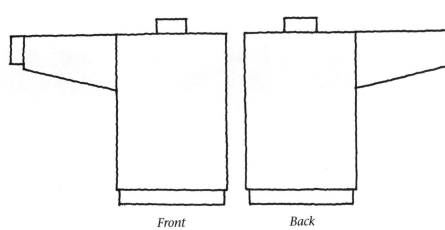

Front   *Back*

134

Sailor

MEASUREMENTS (CHEST SIZES)

Child's, about age six: 76cm/30 in.
(Child's, about age twelve: 100cm/39½ in.)
Medium, woman's: 116cm/45½ in.
(Large, man's: 140cm/55 in.)

NUMBER OF PATTERN REPEATS

12 (16) 18 (22)
(14, 20 or 24 pattern repeats may be used for alternative sizes)

YARN

Fingering-weight yarn
White: 1½ (2) 3 (4) 100g balls [5 oz. (7 oz.) 10½ oz. (14 oz.)]; Blue: 2½ (3) 4 (5) 100g balls [9 oz. (10½ oz.) 14 oz. (18 oz.)]

NEEDLES

1 circular needle in sizes 2½mm (U.S. 1-2, U.K. 12-13) and 3mm (U.S. 2-3, U.K. 11), 1 set of double-pointed needles in sizes 2½mm (U.S. 1-2, U.K. 12-13) and 3mm (U.S. 2-3, U.K. 11) and 1 pair of needles in size 3mm (U.S. 2-3, U.K. 11)

GAUGE

Ribbing: 30 stitches to 10cm/4 in.; two-color stockinette stitch: 28 stitches to 10cm/4 in. It is recommended to knit a gauge sample; should your gauge differ from the one indicated, change to smaller or larger needles.

FRONT AND BACK

Using the smaller circular needle and blue yarn, cast on 200 (261) 290 (356) stitches.

Knitting in the round, knit the ribbing (knit 2, purl 1) for 16 (20) 24 (26) rows.

Change to stockinette stitch and increase the number of stitches by 16 (27) 34 (40) distributed over the row. Knit 3 (3) 4 (4) rows in stockinette stitch.

Change to the larger circular needle and knit the pattern according to the diagram.

Knit 4 (5) 6 (8) repeats of the first pattern (see the photo and diagram), followed by 2 (2) 3 (3) rows in stockinette stitch.

Change to white yarn and knit 1 row (knitwise), followed by 2 (2) 3 (3) rows in moss stitch.

Change to blue yarn and knit 2 (2) 3 (3) rows in stockinette stitch before proceeding to the next two-color pattern, which is knitted in 12 (16) 18 (22) stripe repeats of 18 stitches.

Knit the pattern for 12cm/4½ in. (14cm/5½ in.) 18cm/7 in. (25cm/10 in.) or until the desired length has been achieved.

Divide for front and back, starting at the center of a moss-stitch stripe.

Knit the front for 10cm/4 in. (14cm/5½ in.) 16cm/6 in. (18cm/7 in.)

Place the 7 (9) 15 (23) center stitches onto a spare needle or safety pin. Knit each side separately, casting off every other row:
5-4-3-2-1 (5-4-3-2-1) 5-4-3-2-1 (6-5-4-3-2-1) stitches.

Knit for 4cm/1½ in. (6cm/2 in.) 6cm/2 in. (7cm/2½ in.) without shaping, ending with a purl row from the right side. Put the stitches onto a spare needle or piece of yarn.

Knit the front for 15cm/6 in. (20cm/8 in.) 22cm/8½ in. (24cm/9½ in.).

Place the 23 (25) 31 (43) center stitches onto a spare needle or safety pin. Knit each side separately, casting off every other row: 3-2-1-1 (3-2-1-1) 3-2-1-1 (4-3-2-1-1) stitches.

Knit 1cm/½ in. (2cm/½ in.) 2cm/½ in. (3cm/1 in.) without shaping.

Make sure that the number of shoulder stitches is the same for front and back. End with a purl row from the right side. Put the shoulder stitches back onto a needle. Working from the wrong side, knit together the stitches from the front with those of the back, casting off at the same time.

DIAGRAM FOR FRONT AND BACK

Pattern repeat   *Center side*

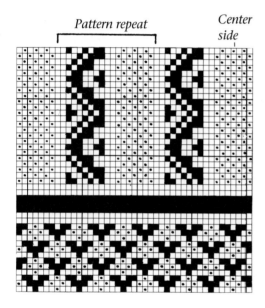

DIAGRAM FOR SLEEVE

Pattern repeat

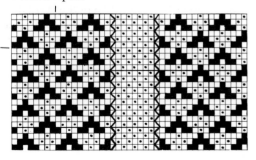

■ = *white*
□ = *blue*
● = *purl stitch*
> = *place for decreasing sleeve*

SLEEVES

Using the smaller double-pointed needles and blue yarn, pick up 102 (126) 142 (158) stitches around the armhole. Make sure the correct gauge (28 stitches to 10cm/4 in.) is maintained.

Knit 2 rows in stockinette stitch, interrupted by a moss-stitch band over 7 stitches to match the moss stitches in the body piece.

Change to the larger double-pointed needles and knit the pattern according to the diagram.

Decrease for the narrowing of the sleeve at each side of the moss-stitch stripe about every 5th row.

When the sleeve measures 27cm/10½ in. (34cm/13½ in.) 42cm/16½ in. (52cm/20½ in.), change back to the smaller double-pointed needles and knit 2 rows in stockinette stitch. If necessary, make a final decrease, distributed over the row, so that 39 (48) 60 (72) stitches remain on the needle.

Knit the ribbing (knit 2, purl 1) for 12 (15) 18 (20) rows. Cast off.

NECKBAND

Using the smaller double-pointed needles and blue yarn, pick up about 94 (120) 134 (180) stitches. Knit the ribbing for 8 (10) 12 (14) rows. Cast off.

137

Mate

MEASUREMENTS (CHEST SIZE)
136cm/53½ in.

YARN
Worsted-weight yarn
12 100g balls [42 oz.]

NEEDLES
1 circular needle in size 3½mm (U.S. 4, U.K. 9-10) and 1 set of double-pointed needles in size 3½mm (U.S. 4, U.K. 9-10)

GAUGE
22 stitches to 10cm/4 in. It is recommended to knit a gauge sample; should your gauge differ from the one indicated, change to smaller or larger needles.

See the instructions for *Rainbow* on p. 112 — *Mate* is knitted in the same way. However, *Mate* has 18 squares of 12 stitches (in the round) and is knitted in a thicker yarn than *Rainbow*, which has 28 squares of 8 stitches.

A reduced or increased number of stitches per square will change the size.

The length of *Mate* (see the photo on p. 134) is 19 squares or 78cm/31 in. The length of the sleeve is 54cm/21½ in.,

and the narrowing has been achieved by knitting 5 squares of 12 stitches, 2 squares of 11, 2 of 10, 2 of 9 and 4½ of 8.

The casting off at the neckline differs from that of *Rainbow* and is done according to the following:

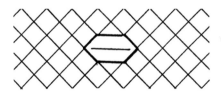

FINISHING
The edges are picked up, using the gauge indicated above, and are knitted in the round in stockinette stitch.

LOWER EDGE
Using the circular needle, pick up about 280 stitches. Knit 16 rows in stockinette stitch, followed by 1 purl row from the right side and another 16 rows in stockinette stitch.

CUFF
Pick up about 60 stitches. Knit in the round, as for the lower edge.

TURTLENECK
Using double-pointed needles, pick up about 110 stitches.

Knit 44 rows in stockinette stitch, followed by 1 purl row from the right side and another 44 rows in stockinette stitch.

Fold the edges to the wrong side at the purl row and slip stitch in place.

Abbreviations

K   = knit
P   = purl (occasionally used and
       explained in context)
st   = stitch
tog = together
yrn = yarn around needle

Yarn and Needle Equivalents

The sample sweaters in this book were knitted with Swedish handknitting and weaving yarns. The instructions for each garment specify both a given number of 100g balls or skeins of yarn and the yarn equivalent in ounces, for those working with coned yarn. The knitting yarns you find available in this country may not be sold in 100g balls but rather in 50g or 25g balls, skeins or hanks; and the amount of yarn in a given ball, skein or hank varies from brand to brand. Thus, consider the yarn amounts indicated for a garment to be approximate, and be careful in your calculations.

Whatever yarn you choose, knit a sample gauge swatch with the needle size suggested by the author to be sure that your gauge is correct. If it is not, change the needle size (or yarn) until your gauge matches the gauge specified for the pattern.

Below are several types of yarn and the approximate gauge they generally yield with the needle size indicated.

If you wish to use Shetland yarn, Jamieson & Smith yarn is available in a wide range of colors, unlike most brands of 100% Shetland yarn.

Jamieson & Smith, Ltd.
90 North Road
Lerwick
Shetland Isles
Scotland, UK
ZE1 OPQ
Phone: 011-33-595-3579

YARN EQUIVALENT CHART

Yarn	Needle size	Stitch gauge (stitches per inch)
Worsted weight	6 to 8	5 to 5½
Double-knitting weight	5 to 6	5½
Sport weight	3 to 5	6 to 6¾
Fingering weight or Shetland yarn	1 to 3	7 to 8¾

NEEDLE EQUIVALENT CHART

Metric	U.S.	U.K.
2mm	0	14
2½mm	1-2	12-13
3mm	2-3	11
3½mm	4	9-10
4mm	5-6	8

From time to time, Jamieson & Smith yarn is available in the U.S. At the time of publication, it was carried by the shops listed below. The range of colors and price may vary from store to store.

Blue Hill Yarns
Box 201
Blue Hill, ME 04614
(207) 374-5631

Dream Weaver
650 Miami Circle NE
Atlanta, GA 30324
(404) 237-4588

Kaleidoscope Yarns
16 Church Street
Belfast, ME 04915
(207) 338-2902

Renee-Yarn
4801 Montgomery Drive
Santa Rosa, CA 95409
(707) 538-1519

Schoolhouse Press
6899 Cary Bluff Road
Pittsville, WI 54466
(715) 884-2799

Tomato Factory Yarn Co.
8 Church Street
Lambertville, NJ 08530
(609) 397-3475

The Wool Shop
25 The Plaza
Locust Valley, NJ 11560
(516) 671-9722

The Wooly West
208 South 13th East
Salt Lake City, UT 84102
(801) 583-9373

Yarn Galore
4614 Wisconsin Avenue NW
Washington, DC 20016
(202) 686-KNIT